Solving History

Solving History:
The Challenge of Environmental Activism

RAYMOND A. ROGERS

BLACK
ROSE
BOOKS

Montréal/ New York/London

Black Rose Books No. AA258
Hardcover ISBN: 1-55164-113-5 (bound)
Paperback ISBN: 1-55164-112-7 (pbk.)
Library of Congress Catalog Card Number: 97-74160

Canadian Cataloguing in Publication Data

Rogers, Raymond Albert
Solving history : the challenge of environmental activism

ISBN 1-55164-113-5 (bound).—
ISBN 1-55164-112-7 (pbk.)

1. Environmentalism. 2. Environmental protection. 3. Economic
development—Environmental aspects. 4. Human ecology. I. Title.

GE195.R64 1998   363.7'05   C97-900736-4

Cover Design by Associés libres, Montréal

**BLACK
ROSE
BOOKS**

C.P. 1258   250 Sonwil Drive   99 Wallis Road
Succ. Place du Parc   Buffalo, New York   London, E9 5LN
Montréal,Québec   14225 USA   England
H2W 2R3 Canada

To order books in North America: (phone) 1-800-565-9523 (fax) 1-800-221-9985
In Europe: (phone) 44-0181-986-4854 (fax) 44-0181-533-5821

Our Web Site address: http://www.web.net/blackrosebooks

A publication of the Institute of Policy Alternatives of Montréal (IPAM)

Printed in Canada

In memory of Egon Czerny (1911–1992)
who said:
"Nature doesn't mind.
It takes such pleasure making new ones."

Acknowledgments

I would like to thank my colleagues in the Faculty of Environmental Studies for giving me an academic home: most especially Paul Wilkinson, John Livingston, Neil Evernden, Mora Campbell, Gerry Daly, and Anita McBride. I wish to thank others for their encouragement and advice: Abraham Rotstein, David MacDonald, John Ferguson, and Ellen Meiksins Wood, as well as members of the *Capitalism Nature Socialism* Toronto editorial group. I also wish to thank Chris Wilkinson for his help in researching this book, as well as Carina Hernandez for her help, along with Margaret Logan and Marek Swinder, in readying it for publication.

Thanks to Catherine Stewart, who was a co-author of an earlier version of the chapter on the Pacific Salmon fishery, which was published in the *American Review of Canadian Studies,* and to Chris Wilkinson again, who did extensive research of an earlier version of the endangered species chapter, which we have submitted to *Policy Studies Journal.* I also wish to thank the Social Science and Humanities Research Council for a grant to aid in the research of this book, and the Research Committee in the Faculty of Environmental Studies at York University for a grant to aid in the preparation of the book for publication. And of course, I want to thank Black Rose Books for their patience and receptiveness, and for sending this work out into the world.

Most of all, I want to thank my mate Laura Jane McLauchlan, and our son Lauchlan, for being who they are, as well as thanks to my family back in Manitoba, and my many friends in Nova Scotia. Hail mortals!

Contents

Preface

*S*olving History is, of course, a contradiction in terms. But so is "sustainable development." Any discussion of conservation in the age of global capitalism seems so rife with contradictions and difficulties, that it appears to be endless bad news with no possibility of hope. So in using the title *Solving History*, I feel that I am tilting the oxymorons in the direction of hope. The focus of *Solving History* is an attempt to highlight the fact that, capitalism itself has a history, and is therefore not the only context in which to understand environmental problems, and that the relations that currently exist are there by our consent, and need not dominate the way we think and act.

More specifically, this book is based on the recognition that conservation of the natural world has little hope of success if analysis and action *assume* capitalism as the frame of reference in which to understand environmental problems. Conservation is a lost cause as long as it is conceived of as a specialty activity operating within the structures and processes of industrial capitalism. In these terms, conservation is an entirely circumscribed afterthought that runs contrary to the metabolism of dominant historical realities, appearing most times as a heavy-handed set of restrictions and regulations which are only effective enough to create "inefficiency" without ever achieving conservation goals. Therefore, a lot of the environmental debate has to do with making conservation more efficient and less heavy-handed, in other words, aligning it with capitalism, rather than setting out ways to make the structures and processes of capital the subject of analysis.

Conservation is inseparable from the social context in which it manifests itself. Viable conservation requires a viable social context. Current movements toward increasing global economic competitiveness — and the consequent lessening of social and political perspectives — do not provide a viable social context for conservation. Therefore the central project for conservation is the challenging of this reduced social standing of humans and nature in terms of resources which support this economic agenda. Viable social relations require an expanded conception of the "political" and the "social" in human-nature relations, and a consequent reduction in the role of market relations. Elected officials who might be expected to take up the mantle of environmental protection increasingly conceive of their role as pavers of the way of the "level playing field" of global capitalism.

In setting out a project in terms of "solving history," this inquiry links a sense of immediacy with one of historicity. The sustainability debate is occurring in a world captivated by the forces of unsustainability, and analytical failure has accompanied ecological failure when it comes to understanding the root causes of unsustainability. It is very clear to me that environmental problems are not about "resolving issues"; they are about coming to terms with particular histories associated with modern economic development, which, in turn, require a challenge directed at specific interests which have been the beneficiaries of that development.

Other species on the Earth appear, most times, as little more than cannon fodder in human history. If environmental concerns have to do with relocating human history within natural history, this work is meant to challenge the impoverishment of separating human history from natural history in the first place. Overcoming this impoverishment is a social project, rather than a technical enterprise associated with carrying capacity. If any world is hard-wired and determined these days, it is certainly not the sociality of undisturbed natural communities, but, rather, it is the economically-determined human behaviour which circumscribes late-modern thought and action.

It is my intention to link "radical" and "practical" perspectives in addressing environmental problems. In taking up the project of "solving history," I am certainly not trying to deny the complexity of the historical process, but rather to recognize that, as Ellen Meiksins Wood states: "In today's world economy ... it may now be more rather than less realistic to think about radical alternatives."[1] The purpose of this book, then, is to engage in a form of analysis which opens up possibility for action and challenge, rather than leading to conclusions which merely confirm the status quo and the closing down of possibility. I believe that this approach is essential to the survival of local human communities and natural communities.

In *The Oceans Are Emptying: Fish Wars and Sustainability*, I engaged in a particular case study of the relationship between conservation and development. *Nature and the Crisis of Modernity: A Critique of Contemporary Discourse on Managing the Earth* set out a general analysis of the historical underpinnings of the relationship between conservation and development in modernity which arose out of the case study of the fishery. It is my intention in this book to link the analysis of the "deep historicity" of environmental problems with the case study practicalities of marginalized groups attempting to save themselves in the here and now of history.

Most "solutions" to environmental problems strategize with variables that are part of these problems without necessarily engaging in a critical analysis of those variables. The conception of sustainability as the "integration" of conservation and development perspectives is a typical example of this type of "solution." I believe that the relationship between conservation and development requires challenge on the part of conservation, rather than integration. Historical forces which are marginalizing human communities and destroying natural communities are aggressively pursuing an intensifying agenda of exploitation and domination. Marginalized groups do not find themselves in benign situations, by definition. Therefore any call for conservation in this context is a call that requires resistance and challenge to current realities, rather than accommodation and integration. The only people for whom this resistance and challenge does not appear as a "practical" response to current historical realities are those who are ensnared in the forces that are destroying us.

The steadfastness of my challenge to the forces of economic development does not arise out of a cranky and dogmatic recalcitrance with regard to life as it is offered, but rather from the recognition that the openness and spontaneity of our world is under threat from an economic rigour that is turning into *rigor mortis*. The only way we can escape these strictures is to take a long step back from the paranoid cliff-edge of ecological collapse which economic development (at its "sustainable" best) condemns us to walk for the rest of history. At its worst, modern economic relations will bring widespread disaster, for which the collapse in Canada's East Coast fishery is only one of many foreshadowings.

The sustainability debate is a temporary and illusory goal arising from an initial recognition that we live in the world of unsustainability. We have flipped the negative condition of "unsustainability" into the positive initiative of "sustainability" with little recognition of the momentum of the historical forces that continue to push us ever onward through the upheavals of social and ecological failure. Conservation, in these terms, is a "faint-hope" project for an offender in need of some very serious rehabilitation.

In his discussion of Leo Tolstoy, John Updike makes the point that the best novels are smarter than the authors who wrote them. This achievement has to do with the inspired wager into uncertainty the author takes up as a challenge in writing the novel, and a vitality which allows him or her to fulfill the wager. Generally speaking, I believe that the opposite is the case with regard to our wagered "output" in late modern society: our world is coarser and crueler than we are as individuals. Less and less is being asked of us as human beings. In order to deal with a range of environmental woes now confronting us, it may be that we will have to live collective lives more inspired than is currently the case.

NOTE

1   Ellen Meiksins Wood. 1995. *Democracy Against Capitalism: Renewing Historical Materialism*. New York: Cambridge University Press, p. 290.

I

Conservation and the
Darkening Hue of Development

The environmental fight has to be fought in the heart of modern economy, not in the extremities of the environmental movement. To fight the environmental fight in the heart of modern economy does not mean to accept the terms of reference set by modern economy. Rather, the central goal of conservation is to challenge the assumptions of modern economy, as well as the goals and processes which arise from those assumptions. To accept a limited environmental agenda which operates as a kind of "add-on" to the forces of development — as well as accepting development's current conception of the "political" and "economic" spheres — is to doom conservation of the natural world to a rapidly accelerating failure. At the beginning of a six-hundred-page study entitled *The Philosophy of Money*, Georg Simmel makes the statement that "not a single line of this investigation is meant to be a statement about economics."[1] Similarly, this inquiry examines "modern development" without accepting the assumptions which inform these historical forces.

The perception that the focus of environmentalism has to be directed at the structures and processes at the heart of capitalism arises most clearly from the peripheral positions such as the one occupied by Atlantic Canadian fishing communities. It is this polarity which informs the organization and intent of this book. First, capitalism must be challenged at its centre, not fobbed off to a limited agenda within the environmental movement. Second, this recognition presents itself with the greatest urgency and clarity in peripheral areas such as Canada's East Coast fishing industry, and most directly with regard to marginalized inshore fishers in coastal communities. Analytic centrality is linked, then, with a spatial and regional marginality in this analysis of the political economy of depletion and dependence.[2]

There is a kind of beholding, along with the misery, which is offered to those who experience things from an engaged marginality. The margin is a particularly useful vantage point for environmental concerns because it provides an anchor into a perspective on the world which is at odds with the dominant one. This allows for a more evocative recognition that what may appear as the "objectivity of the present" is a cobbled-together historical artifact which — although it has its own internal logic which captures those who are immersed in it — is viewed from the margin as a set of relations whose authority is open to question. It is this contrast in perspectives which informs a great deal of inter-cultural debate between Northern and Southern countries concerning environmental issues, and it is this inter-cultural debate which informs the relationship between Ottawa and Atlantic coastal communities in the context of the collapse of the fishing industry.

Coastal communities exist where they do in Atlantic Canada because of their role as outposts of the British and French empires. The pursuit of riches, dislocation back home, a place in the colonial order, rather than an attachment to the natural world, were the motivations which brought people to these coastal communities. But situations change: empires collapse, people move on, out of reluctance as much as ambition. Or people grow attached to a place, as hard as the life might be. It is the unlikeliest of things sometimes, which come to pass. It was never the plan but here people are spread out in small coastal communities, holding on now in the aftermath of ecological collapse as they have held on so many times before. It is what these people have given themselves over to which divides them from the centre now. The retraining programs are designed for the newly-stupid, made so by the intrusion of experts in the management process and over-exploitation in the industrial process. And the way out now, in the circumstances of depletion and dependence, the stupidest of conditions? Stay in the place the world tries to talk you out of? Institutionalize the marginality? Challenge the stupidity and denigration?

Wolfgang Sachs has referred to modern economic development as an "intellectual ruin."[3] Given the chronic depletion and dependence which hectors marginalized areas — and the connection this depletion and dependence has with standard practice in a modern economy — what is becoming increasingly clear is that current resource management and sustainability strategies are trying to patch up a disaster with a ruin. Such is the state of historical realities which inform current environmental policy making. The challenge this inquiry takes up is the creation of a perspective which is not implicated in this intellectual ruin, and therefore offers some hope to marginalized human communities and surviving natural communities.

In these terms, what has to be challenged is the increasingly narrow conception of politics which has evolved in capitalist relations by arguing for an expanded conception of the political realm which can include the politics of appropriation and domination buried in the economy. An activist agenda which does not take on the increasing privatization of political power in the economic sphere severely circumscribes its realm of activity, and does not address the processes of domination and appropriation in the private economic sphere which cause environmental problems.

This privatization of political power is underwritten by the twin abstractions related to pumping surplus labour out of humans and surplus resources out of nature. These abstract categories of exploitation have taken on what Georg Lukács calls a "phantom objectivity" in capitalism, thereby confirming the domination of commodities in modern life.[4] The categories of surplus labour in humans and surplus resources in nature are phantasms that only exist on balance sheets and in the minds of those who think in ways that confirm the processes of domination and appropriation in capitalism. In other words, these categories are inextricably connected to the buried politics in modern market economy. It is the interconnectedness of this triad which forms the analytical focus of this book: the privatized politics in modern economy impoverishes conceptions of human identity and conceptions of nature by rendering them in terms that suit the expansion of capital. Ensnarement in the abstractions undermines any worthwhile analysis of environmental problems because it renders capitalism invisible.

This project of "solving history," then, can be described as one which externalizes those realities which had hitherto been internal to "economic development" (externalizing internalities rather than internalizing externalities), thereby depicting them in ways that open up the possibility for an expanded conception of historical trajectory underwritten by an expanded political realm, as well as an expanded and interactive sense of "the social" which links human and nature in interactive terms, rather than having humans and nature exist as the passive material of economic development.

To focus on issues such as the social constructions of nature or biocentric conceptions of human identity without recognizing that these areas of study are connected to, and indeed, created by relations in capitalism is to deflect analysis away from the deep historicity of environmental problems and to valorize categories which are part of the problem. Once again, the environmental fight has to be fought in the heart of modern economy.

To those critics who would claim that pursuing these initiatives is an unreasonable project, all I can reply is that it does not seem so to those who suffer dislocation and marginalization at the hands of current historical initiatives linked to increasing global economic competitiveness. To take on the project of "solving history," then, is to preserve the opportunity that there might be other historical trajectories — both for natural communities and human communities — than the increasingly totalizing and homogenizing path of industrial capitalism. This attempt to preserve the opportunity for other historical trajectories arises out of the recognition that the increasing dominance of market relations is inherently antagonistic to a co-evolving sense of the relationship between local human culture and natural habitat.

Those who show concern about environmental issues do so because, in general, they are said to "care" about these issues. This caring runs contrary to the sense that, increasingly, the dominant forces in our world don't "care," or at least if there is "care," it is a particularly negative interest that is taken in terms of exploitation. Capitalism does not care, except in this negative sense. At the heart of modern culture is a set of relations and forces that do not care in any positive manner. In expanding the political into the realm of the economic, and in externalizing the opportunity for meaning in the world by linking human history with natural history, I am proposing a kind of caring where there currently is very little of it. Not that there was a time when "care" was the organizing quality in the world, although, indeed, that may be necessary now. But there was a co-evolving sense of participatory inter-dependence which was always being re-negotiated in an experiential way, as opposed to the one-way mirror of economic interests which dominates the world now. Given the precarious state of the biosphere these days, counseling for increased caring of the non-economic kind cannot be far off the mark, but is useless unless it grapples with the forces which cause environmental problems.

In recognizing that capitalism does not "care," I am asking many of us to do the hardest thing: to make ourselves vulnerable in an increasingly meaner world. It may seem easier to merely duck in an expedient way and hope that disaster arrives at someone else's door and not our own. Louis Sass refers to this as a "devitalized condition" in which there is an increasing fear expressed about threatening aspects of a world which can be compared to a psychopath who uses:

> displays of lack of feeling — a jokey, chilling indifference
> to subjects that normally evoke strong emotions — to gain
> control of others and make them feel vulnerable. If others
> show their revulsion, their vulnerability becomes obvious;
> if they do not show it, they have been compelled to dis-
> semble, thus tacitly confirming the bully's power.[5]

It is this double bind that has been created by the discipline and surveillance of capitalism: face denigration or defeat. As bleak as it may seem, generating a challenge to dominant forces out of this weak position holds out the most hope. Generating the kind of initiatives required to address conservation issues from a more comfortable position within current economic and technological realities has not succeded. The hopes of that enlightenment project of conservation through education and information are gone. It is left now to the margins, especially those margins where the grip of these modern realities have slackened because profit seekers have moved on, to create a social project which offers some hope.

I use terms such as "metaphors of care" or "moral economy" not as a "do-good" project, but one that recognizes the challenge required to the deep historicity and specificity of the relations which brought about the dire situation in which we find ourselves. If we are to break the totalizing power of capitalism without undue upheaval and suffering, we need to reclaim a broader social realm which is currently circumscribed by economic rationality.

MANICURING THE MONSTER

The process of "patching up a disaster with a ruin" and the displacement and denigration which usually accompanies it is illustrated by the recent and repeated attacks by organizations such as the *Toronto Globe and Mail* on the compensation payments to East Coast fishers who were adversely affected by the fishing moratorium declared in 1992 by the Federal Department of Fisheries and Oceans for large areas of the Atlantic continental shelf. The conceptual counterpart to "patching up a disaster with a ruin" is "analytical failure following on from ecological failure." This analytical failure is expressed in arguments which are all but universal and which state that the problems in the fishery have to do with the fact that the fishery is not "capitalist enough" because it does not have fully developed private property rights. For example, the *Globe and Mail* claims that "the industry should be based on individuals holding quotas. These quotas (or ITQs [Individual Transferable Quotas]) can then be traded … so that the fishery becomes a fully-property-based regime."[6] In order to drive this point home, Garrett Hardin's "tragedy of the commons" metaphor is paraphrased in comparing the private-property-based agriculture industry with the common-property aspects of the fishery:

> Suppose that in the last century Ottawa had not given away the fertile Western prairies to settlers and railways, but had instead kept them, making them freely accessible to all. Each year farmers line up, awaiting the signal from Ottawa. When the starting gun is fired, each may rush out and plant, during a government defined planting season, anywhere where someone else has not already planted, up to a government dictated maximum.[7]

This "thought experiment" argues that private property has provided a basis for success in Prairie farming, while common property in the fishery has been an administrative and economic nightmare. The lessons the fishery can therefore learn from farmers is that privatization of fish quota will promote "technological innovation," "improved yields," and "careful stewardship."

I grew up in a small Prairie town in southwestern Manitoba and many of my family are still farming in the area. As an young adult, I settled on the south shore of Nova Scotia and spent a good part of my working life as a full-time commercial fisherman. I come away from this life experience having learned very different lessons from the ones outlined in such editorials. As I see them, the problems in the fishery are not due to "market failure" caused by government subsidies and lack of property rights. They are caused by a "human failure" to provide an ethical, social, and ecological context in which to understand the ramifications of economic and technological domination in our lives. What I experienced in farming and fishing is the concentration of corporate power and vertical integration of food production, leading to the depletion of soils and fish stocks, the disappearance of small communities, the undermining of the cooperative food buying systems, and the collapse of the family farm and inshore owner/operators as the social unit which supported these institutions.

It is possible to argue that, because of changes in technological capability and economic requirements, there was necessarily a change in labour requirements and settlement patterns related to food production, and that farming has managed this adaptation with less government support than the fishery because of private property rights. But the larger implications behind these changes have to do not with merely adapting to economic and technological changes, but with asking the question: "What is society for, anyway?"

There is no doubt that common property is anathema to industrial production in the fishery, and that the family farm has no ethical, moral standing within current agri-business schemes, but it is necessary to consider what form of human community *is* adapted to current economic and technological requirements. I think what is becoming clear is that not only is common property anathema to industrial production, but that viable conceptions of human community (with health care, education, pensions, for example) and healthy natural communities also run contrary to the requirements of an increasingly globalized economy. Instead, we have the Department of Human Resources reflecting a redefinition of human identity as raw material for industrial production, and a Department of Natural Resources which sees nature as so much industrial "throughput," thereby conveying the increasingly dominant position of capital and technology and a reduced social standing for humans and nature.

It is therefore appropriate that the *Globe and Mail* editorial uses Hardin's community-less, culture-less, impoverished being in the "thought experiment" for how humans behave, as individual freedom leads to collective ruin in the "tragedy of the commons" metaphor: replete with men who "rush" about in ever "faster, more powerful tractors" because no one "would care for the land" because one "could never be sure if he would be farming the same piece of ground next year." But is this not precisely the kind of free market behaviour which we reward in our society? Is it not what is currently being institutionalized in the context of economic globalization? These imperatives sound more like stock market behaviour, than any farming or fishing community I know. It sounds like proselytizing on behalf of trans-national corporations who are cutting a wide swath across the resources of the Southern Hemisphere, while enjoying the government supports for the good life in the North.

By presenting private property as a kind of salve which will lead to fishers engaging in "careful stewardship," or at least to being "better off" by "selling out," the editorial engages in an analytical "sleight-of-hand" which would lead us to believe that all is well and good in market economy, and all is wrong with what has supported coastal communities in the past. In doing so, the "get with the program" approach uses a form of analysis which further entrenches the economic and technological forces which are already surpassing global ecological limits, and achieves this by denigrating the relations which do not fit into that historical momentum.

The "cut and run" mentality dominated the fishery while there were still fish to catch, as it does in the global economy currently. I haven't read any GATT documents recently calling for increased autonomy and control of resources for Southern countries in the name of better stewardship. This would threaten Northern industrial profits. Once the resources are depleted and local communities are vulnerable, calls for autonomy and rationality by opinion makers such as the *Globe and Mail* seem to be little more than a mopping-up exercise as economic concerns move on to "greener" pastures.

There is no doubt that Canadian taxpayers have unduly subsidized the fishery for far too long — in corporate restructuring as well as through unemployment insurance payments — but to assume that the extension of property rights will solve this problem is to fail to recognize that the increased individual rationality which we associate with private property's role in industrial society has resulted in a collective inappropriateness in global ecological terms. In overcoming this inappropriateness, what is required is the reclaiming of social standing for humans and nature by challenging the increasing privatization of political and social power in the global economy.

This reclaiming of social standing runs contrary to the recent history of conservation where it is clear that environmental policy initiatives take their cues from economic development priorities. The history of environmental policy is a history of *responses* to the appearance of environmental problems which are, in turn, generated by the priorities of industrial exploitation. It is a game of musical chairs. Every time the music stops the economic domination has intensified, and there are fewer species and habitat, and there are fewer structures and processes (and corresponding conceptions of human identity) which can be called upon in the name of conservation. Then the music starts up again, and there is a ceremony in which some new title of a "more efficient" conservation agenda is trotted out such as Ontario's "Lands For Life" forestry initiative, which allows for large sections of Ontario's forests to be leased to forestry companies in the name of good forestry management. The music has turned to a dirge by now, and only the most zealous toadies can muster any enthusiasm for the few remaining seats allotted to conservation.

The forces of economic development provide rationales for expanding their authority. In the creation of a response, environmental policy constructs a conception of what problem it is addressing, and the relation that problem has to the larger socio-political context. This process has led to a profound shrinking in the mandates offered to conservation practitioners as their activities are redefined by the priorities for development. Thus, the interest that is taken in the natural world is increasingly a negative interest linked to the requirements of development. Because of this dependent status as a kind of "add-on" to development, conservation measures are many times implicated in this negative interest, and offer little hope of any long-term success.

CONSERVATION, CAPITALISM, AND COMMUNITY

> Properly speaking, there is no "crisis of biological diversity" or even an "ecological crisis." But there is a large and growing political crisis that has ecological and other consequences.
>
> David Orr[8]

Given the increasing dominance of capitalism in our world, it becomes very difficult to recognize that capitalism itself has a history, that at every stage in its evolution, humans have had extensive discussions about the social good of expanding capitalist relations. What strikes me about current discussions of extending the institutionalization of capitalism through privatization, deregulation, and free trade is that those who support these initiatives feel that the logic of their initiatives is self-evident and does not require discussion — as if these initiatives were some kind of default position of humanity — while those who oppose them are fractured and weak, and are unable to find a viable perspective from which to oppose these initiatives. And if they do, these challenges don't seem to generate much public debate.

The indifference of most people in industrialized society to this debate, and to environmental issues generally, is directly connected to relations in capitalism, not just in terms of their pervasiveness but also in the way they invert the world, so that we seem to be dominated by the realities of profit and accumulation, as if these were things in and of themselves, rather than human creations. In order to develop a form of analysis which does not merely confirm current relations, leading to acceptance and resignation, the project of "solving history" highlights that, indeed, current relations have a history, and there exists the opportunity to resist their totalization, thereby leading to a recognition that humans can still "make" history, rather than just laying down and surrendering to the "logic" of economic and technological expansion.

Marshall Sahlins states that while "history is culturally ordered," it is also the case that "cultural schemes are historically ordered."[9] Operating between these two realities is the "creative action of the historic subjects, the people concerned." Within this scripted interaction, it nonetheless remains possible for people to "creatively reconsider their conventional schemes," thereby leading to a "structural transformation" of historical relations. It is this active and creative response to the practicalities of current relations which is required if we are to address conservation issues in a viable way.

Most of my time is occupied with teaching courses whose main focus is the conservation of the natural world. After taking into consideration the various strategies set out for conservation, I arrive at the end of the day with a sense that conservation seems to be a black box with no doors. Whether it is the importance of environmental education, childhood experience, public-private relations of the policy community, round table initiatives, relations between conservation and development, the internalization of externalities, environmental thought, equity issues, political economy analysis, the role of science in policy making, the call for interdisciplinary research, one can't help but be struck by the fact it all seems insufficient, given the retreats and failures that are occurring on all sides.

Attempts to solve the problems in the fishery, for example, by increasing the efficiency and rationality of exploitation through the institution of ITQs is emblematic of the fact that initiatives seems to be on an analytic and strategic auto-pilot, even in the face of such obvious disaster, to the point where debate appears futile. My exasperation with myself as I repeat the contrary arguments to development is only exceeded by my exasperation with the pro-development arguments, which, despite what I would regard as many direct hits being landed in the name of conservation, the development arguments bob back up like weighted targets in a circus sideshow.

In more overtly political terms, what is clear is that governments are now entirely preoccupied with doing the bidding of the economic forces that are destroying human communities and natural communities. Those who are concerned with viable human relations and viable human-nature relations will have to challenge these forces in the name of their own survival and an expanded democracy, all the time preserving or discovering the fact that there are alternatives to the current forces which dominate our world.

OVERCOMING OPPOSITIONS

In setting out this project from a social perspective, it is my intention to make problematic the separation of the economic from political, of human meaning from collective experience, and of human history from natural history. In the first case, a social perspective on relations in capitalism challenges the separation of the economic and political spheres by arguing that a great deal of the political power in capitalism has been privatized in the economic sphere. Rather than being seen in their political aspect as social relations between humans, the economic sphere is presented in terms of a logic which is drained of its political content. It is here where economic relations generate the reified categories of exploitation whereby surplus labour is pumped out of direct producers and surplus resources are pumped out of nature. For there to be viable social relations, the economic sphere has to be reclaimed as a site of politics which can be influenced by a wider conception of democracy.

Second, a social perspective on the relationship between interior human meaning and the exterior world highlights that with the increasing domination of economic valuation in modernity and the expansion of capitalist discipline in defining human behaviour, humans have lost a sense of the reciprocal social inter-relationship between interiority and exteriority. I would argue that meaning is not always internal and repressed, but may be external and gone. Rather than internal meaning existing as a defensive retreat from an increasingly inhospitable world, a social perspective reclaims the world as a location of viable social negotiation between humans, as well as the recognition of the sociality which underwrites human-nature relations.

Third, a social perspective would reject the idea that, as humans began to gather in Neolithic settlements and domesticate animals and plant crops, they created a social existence in culture with no sense that these newly acculturated humans brought anything social with them, as it were, from their millennia of experience in natural history. By contrast, I argue that nature is a profoundly social place, and it is this social legacy which has continued to sustain us in the increasingly impoverished economic and technological relations in "culture."

Viable conservation measures require the addressing of these social projects. In short, the creation of a social project for humans and nature in opposition to capitalism and technology allows for a redefinition of human relations and human/nature relations. In taking on these projects, conservation therefore has to challenge, or "solve," some of the dominant realities of industrial society.

INDUSTRIAL INTRANSIGENCE AND THE DISENFRANCHISEMENT OF THE POWERFUL

> The unfettered hegemony of Western productivism has made it more and more impossible to take exit roads from the global racetrack.
>
> Wolfgang Sachs[10]

> ... [G]overning institutions have developed a complex repertoire of *responsibility- and crisis-displacement strategies*, thereby preserving their legitimacy with respect to environmental issues while in fact failing to engage in the collective, interstate responses necessary to address crisis tendencies that are inherently global in nature.
>
> Colin Hay[11]

The "crisis-displacement strategies" used by the modern state with regard to environmental issues are, for Hay, the "the single major factor preventing a global response to a global crisis."[12] In contrast to the self-conscious goals of the consultative and collaborative policy making which dominate "enlightened" approaches to conservation in multi-stakeholder round-table processes, Hay argues that there are a "multitude of conflicting state interests that clearly militate against the emergence of such collective responses to environmental crisis."[13] What are we to make of the contrast between the goals of policy makers whose self-conscious project is to engage in a collaborative and consultative process which integrates a range of points of view — as set out in ecosystem initiatives, for example — and Hay's claim that it is the nation-state's relations to this same "multitude" of conflicting interests which is the "single major factor" preventing resolution of these issues?

The explanation for this contradiction lies in the defining aspects of capitalism: namely, in the increasing privatization of political processes in the economy; and the consequent loss of any viable role for government in protecting the "public good." This privatization of the political realm in the economy leads to the shrinking of the realm of public policy and the expansion of the "rationality" of business interests. This encroachment has led to a situation where it is hard to find a politician in the world today who does not conceive of his or her role in facilitating the increasing domination of economic relations. In effect, it is the self-conscious goal of politicians to render themselves irrelevant. It is a massive abdication which has necessitated the rise of New Social Movements which recognize that their interests are threatened in a world dominated by economic interests, and who generally feel that recourse to public policy processes is futile. In ecological terms, what is clear is that, for all the ambitiousness of processes such as ecosystem planning, almost none of it is becoming institutionalized in any meaningful way, and, in fact, the opposite is the case: there is a dismantling of regulatory capability because it interferes with the workings of the market.

The enlightened, interdisciplinary, collaborative, holistic, multi-stakeholder approach acknowledges the range of participants involved in a particular issue without offering an analytical framework which would identify the deep historicity of the various interests involved in environmental issues: an analysis which, in turn, would challenge power relations underwriting current interests who cause environmental degradation, and social and economic injustice. These predatory positions therefore remain at the table, as it were, and given the power these positions wield in the larger world, they do not necessarily act "in good faith" (to put it mildly) in the creation of environmental policy.

In *Democracy Against Capitalism: Renewing Historical Materialism*, Ellen Meiksins Wood sets out the social project of historical materialism within a range of debates concerning the current state of socialism and Marxist social theory. Although only tangentially concerned with ecological issues, what is so striking about Wood's characterization of the dominant forces of capitalism is that it is all but identical to the forces causing current ecological crises. Wood states that:

> The first principle of historical materialism is ... the organization of material life and social reproduction. Class enters the picture when access to the conditions of existence and to the means of appropriation are organized in class ways, that is when some people are systematically compelled by differential access to the means of production or appropriation to transfer surplus labour to others.[14]

The coercion of this set of relations resides in the privatized control of production and appropriation, rather than in extra-economic coercion. Wood states:

> The separation of the political and the economic in capitalism means the separation of communal life from the organization of production ... And political life in capitalism is separated from the organization of exploitation ... At the same time capitalism also brings production and appropriation together in an inseparable unity ... and both these processes ... have been privatized.[15]

In this context, a one-sentence definition of the conditions of capitalism are — in terms of an appropriate double negative — the lack of nonmarket access to the means of subsistence. In other words, capitalism exists when people have to use the market to sustain themselves by having the process of living pass through the privatized structures of production and appropriation. In fact, one can argue that it is the goal of capitalism to force people to both sell their labour and buy their goods through the market, because it is only when this happens that the political institutions of capitalism which privatize property and wealth can operate, and this extension of the market is precisely what is happening to North-South relations in the context of economic globalization.

If there is to be a viable social project which can provide a basis for viable conservation, if there is to be a recognition of the significance of global problems as they manifest themselves in terms of the day to day relations in people's lives, it is essential to see that the goals of capitalism and the causes of global ecological problems are identical. The global ecological crisis is not an aberration, it is a direct result of the structures and processes of modern industrial capitalism.

In order to promote ecological viability, then, it is not that capitalism has to be altered in its *economic* logic through the use of market indicators, it is that capitalism has to challenged in terms of appropriation and domination, that is, in how it operates in *political* terms. Through the privatization of wealth and property, capitalist relations have circumscribed the political realm by burying most of it in the private economic realm. It is this private economic realm which drives appropriation and domination — mainly through trans-national corporations — and if global ecological crises are to be addressed, it will be necessary to reclaim that private economic realm as an appropriate field of political action in an expanded sense of economic as well as political democracy.

ON BECOMING SUPERSTITIOUS: PIERCING THE ARMOUR OF MODERNITY

> Character is from the point of view of the psychoanalyst a
> sort of abnormality, a kind of mechanization of a particular
> way of reaction.
>
> Sandor Ferenczi[16]

The foul fiend bites my back.

Tom a Bedlam in King Lear[17]

What is called consciousness is what has been taken over by the concerns of the world. "Experience" is a historical artifact which reflects more about our times than it does about "us." It so happens that most of the day-to-day activities of the late modern world are increasingly defined by the constructs of modern technology and economics, and the intervention by these forces is almost a benchmark for that "experience." What is left, what is not claimed and organized by the world, is hived off as unconscious.

By becoming a fisherman on the North Atlantic, I avoided a lot of these benchmarks. A usual response to a sense of threat for an urban person is to pull up one's collar and hurry along home. A sense of threat drives us indoors, as it were. But this is exactly what you can't do if you are by yourself out in the North Atlantic in the middle of the night in thick fog. There is no hunkering down here. Despite the elevated level of dread caused by staying outdoors, attention must be paid to the powerful forces that surround you, underwritten as they are by the endless roll and pitch of waves. So rather than the very frame of reality being defined by human creations like technology, as it is most times in urban life, the movement of the waves provides a basis for experience which is anything but a human creation. Human gestures on the ocean move in and out between the larger and more powerful forces of the natural world, and in general, these gestures confine themselves to fear and thanks as they operate within the broader scheme of things. Fear and thanks are larger than the devices of the day, be they radar, sonar, or fiberglass. The range of human experience is broader than rational use of the device paradigm.

The marine world that lays claim to consciousness is a different one from the organized and regulated one linked to human constructs. Like all hunter-gatherers, I had a passive sense of my role in wind and water. This was especially true when it came to catching fish. You never knew what was going to come up on the end of a hook, or if anything would. It was as if the elements were the sensory world on top of the water, and "the deep" was an unconscious but closely connected world out of which came the catch. Or it didn't come. God knows. Fear and thanks. Fins and tails. Hunter or prey? "The weather's so fine, you could go to the West Indies in a tea cup."

Aliveness is not inside us. We are inside aliveness. Living out of doors. Decorum in this situation focuses on yield and plea. "Never wear gray mittens." "Don't turn a bucket upside down aboard the boat." "When your time comes, your time comes." The wager of diligence and attention to detail will only get you part of the way.

In her essay "Human Vulnerability and the Experience of Being Prey," Val Plumwood describes being pulled from a canoe by a crocodile while paddling through Kadadu National Park in Australia:

> A subjectively-centred framework capable of sustaining action and purpose must, I think, view the world "from the inside", structured so as to sustain the concept of an invincible, or at least a continuing, self; we remake the world in that way as actionable, investing it with meaning, reconceiving it as sane, survivable ... The lack of fit between the subject-centred version ... and an "outside" version of the world comes into play in extreme moments ... In that flash when my consciousness had to know the bitter certainty of its end [in being attacked by a crocodile], I glimpsed the world for the first time "from the outside", as no longer my world ... indifferent to my will and struggle, to my life as to my death.[18]

Barely surviving three attacks by the crocodile, Plumwood struggles up a muddy bank and tries to make her way back to the ranger station: "struggl[ing] on through driving rain, shouting for mercy from the sky, apologizing to the angry crocodile, calling out my repentance to this, its place, for the fault of my intrusion." Reflecting later on the experience after she had recovered, Plumwood surmises that the event:

> ... presented to me a lesson about the vulnerability of humankind known still, I think, to certain indigenous cultures,

but lost to the technological one which now colonizes the earth ... [A]s the experience of being prey is eliminated from the face of the earth, along with it goes something it has to teach about the power and resistance of nature and the delusions of human arrogance.[19]

As Norman O. Brown argues, whereas Martin Luther was aware that the monster (the devil) was rampant in the world, the triumph of the modern economy led to a denial that this was the case, which in turn gave the monster an even freer reign because his existence was denied.[20] Possessive individual is achieved as much through what it denies, as what it aspires to, and in its assertiveness, it takes on a larger passivity as embodied capital.

It is my intention to link the privatization of relations in the economic realm with the internalization of experience within the private individual. Possessive individualism has underwritten the expansion of capitalism throughout the modern period and these two processes are, for all intents and purposes, synonymous. It is therefore impossible to challenge one without challenging the other. Both involve an internalization of relations which renders them in the service of the work discipline of capitalism and therefore inaccessible to questions regarding social relations (the participation of objects rather than the participation of subjects).

The source of industrial intransigence as it has operated within the "enlightened" process of multi-stakeholder negotiation in environmental policy making has to do with a form of displacement in epistemological terms, which precedes the displacement strategies regarding environmental crises by nation-states. This epistemological displacement — which penetrates the assumptions of modern economic behaviour — could be called "the disenfranchisement of the powerful." The idea of "disenfranchisement" refers to two myths which are central to the standard practice of environmental policy making and to the enlightenment project generally. The first myth is that there are two separate spheres in modern society: the public sphere in which government-sponsored legislation — operating on the basis of rule of law and equity — sets about making laws in the best interest of society. In reality the membrane which separates these spheres is a porous one through which the edicts of capital pass. Therefore, the environmental policy process is entirely dominated by the forces which generate inequity and overexploitation, and therefore are contrary to viable environmental policy making.

The second myth is that there is a rational, independent individual — as constructed within the forces of modernity — who is making these policy decisions. A case can be made for the exact opposite situation. Modern realities are dominated by inverted relations whereby it is commodities which have the dominant social relations, which humans and nature increasingly serve in material terms. Individuals do well in modern society to the extent that they agree to serve the interests of capital and technology. In other words, they willingly agree to disenfranchise themselves so that they can take up positions as the servants to the expansion of capital.

Of course, this is not how these individuals see the social contract they have signed, because they have reified the world in terms that present their decisions as eminently rational. This reification of the world in terms that suit capital and technology renders any ability to engage in "enlightened" negotiation — which would circumscribe that world and acknowledge interests other than economic ones — as moot before it begins. Modern society rewards those who become the servants of capital with wealth, prestige, and power. First and foremost, environmental conflicts are about conflicts of world views, and it is naive in the extreme to think that the world view of capital and technology will be negotiated away in an "enlightened" manner through collaborative policy making. Only by challenging the phantom objectivity of surplus labour which has siphoned off human relations into the economic realm can an enfranchised political realm be reclaimed.

THE FACE OF THE EARTH: HUMAN HISTORY AND NATURAL HISTORY

Nine-tenths of the living world is beyond a fracture no empathy can cross.

W. H. Auden[21]

> ... nothing much can be done, nothing much can even be
> said, until we are able to see the causes of this ... separa-
> tion of nature from human activity.
>
> Raymond Williams[22]

A principal goal of this book is to assess the consequences of the "fracture" Auden refers to as it relates to environmental concerns, and to accept the challenge of setting out what kind of collective "empathy" might double-back across this fracture in social terms. Emphasizing the metaphor of a fracture to describe environmental issues is a recognition that environmental concerns emanate from a collective sense that there has been a disruption to meaning and experience which has to be addressed if we are going to deal with environmental problems. This disruption — or "interference" as Raymond Williams call it — did not tear the fabric of some idealized harmony between humans and nature which preceded the appearance of capitalism. Rather, what was disrupted was a co-evolving dynamic which moved back and forth between the various realities which could be defined in terms of a natural history. What has occurred in the context of disruption is the emergence of a human history in which the co-evolving sense of natural history is replaced by the domination of a single factor in the process: that is, by the increasing primacy of human exploitation beginning with the Neolithic period, but reaching an increasing singularity in the emergence of "economic development." The sidelining of co-evolution, which was an interactive dynamic not unduly privileging a particular group, has both a political dimension and an ecological dimension.

Marshall Sahlins presents a similar co-evolving dynamic in anthropological terms which has been marginalized by the increasing domination of current historical categories. Sahlins claims that "culture is ... a gamble played with nature [where] ... the effects of such risks can be radical innovations ... to the extent that people, as they are socially enabled, cease to be slaves of their concepts and become their masters."[23] The modern fracture between human history and natural history is underwritten by the reduction in standing of both humans and nature. The replacement of an activity called natural history with what we today might call "scientific" analysis — denying as it did the complex weave of fables, stories, and divinations which linked the world of nature with the human world in an ongoing process — marks a period of intensifying objectivity of both humans and nature by the forces of modern production. To speak of natural communities then, as separate from human communities is to replicate the separation of the political from the economic and the separation of the individual from a wider community. To speak of nature is to confirm culture. The more nature is exploited — the more nature is mixed with culture — the more impoverished becomes the cultural understanding of nature within culture. In these terms, I would include the separation of natural history and human history within what Sahlins calls the "radical binary contrasts by which culture and history are usually thought":

> past and present, static and dynamic, system and event, infrastructure and superstructure, and others of that intellectual, dichotomous ilk. These oppositions are not only phenomenally misleading, I conclude, but analytically debilitating. They are debilitating if only because other civilizations have better understood their synthesis, and in different ways thus synthesize their historical practice. We have to recognize theoretically, find the conceptual place of, the past in the present, the superstructure in the infrastructure, the static in the dynamic, change in stability.[24]

Therefore, a synthesis of natural history and human history is not just a melding of the two, but an overcoming of debilitation in the process. Both are impoverished by their separation, where nature is the passive "ground" upon which human history occurs:

> The heretofore obscure histories of remote islands deserve a place alongside the self-contemplation of the European past — or the history of "civilizations" for their own remarkable contributions to an historical understanding. We thus multiply our conceptions of history by the diversity

of structures. Suddenly, there are all kinds of new things to consider.[25]

If there was ever a case of unwarranted "self-contemplation" in the context of "civilizations," it is the continued primacy of the forces of economic development in the the analysis of environmental problems. What is required, instead, is simultaneously a political and a methodological project in which "there are all kinds of new things to consider."

A corollary to the separation of human history and natural history is the ongoing scientific professionalization of those who engage in biophysical analysis, and the consequent marginalization of the amateur naturalists engaged in natural history, thereby creating a class of "insiders" who had access to new forms of knowledge, and "outsiders" who do not separate the description of nature from their experience of it. In other words, "outsiders" included an animated sense of themselves in what they described, whereas "insiders" relied on the objective scientific gaze drained of affection and attachment. These "insiders" were increasingly ensnared within the "development paradigm" and provided a basis for self-conscious withdrawal from natural history. Most of the science that supports the sustainability debate did not arise of the demands for "good science," but instead arose to meet the needs of industry which required the magic number of "exploit to here and stop, here is the principal and here is the interest in nature." This is a number which may suit the requirements of industry, but it is nowhere to be found in natural processes. Like the category of surplus labour, the category of surplus resources is an abstraction which has to be seen for what it is: an impoverished conceit which confirms exploitation, rather than a conservation category which challenges it.

OUTLINE OF CHAPTERS

This book is motivated by a transformative activism rather than a strategic reformist approach to environmental issues. If a reformist approach accepts current historical realities as a given and strategizes with those givens, the Introduction began by calling into question the analytical frames and rote behaviour which are hostage to current historical assumptions associated with capitalism, and took on the project of beginning to map what kinds of understanding and action are necessary to begin the process.

Chapters Two, Three, Four, and Five focus on the privatization of political power in the economy, the relation between morality and economy, the pumping of surplus labour out of humans, and the pumping of surplus resources out of nature. Chapter Two examines the significance of capitalist relations in terms of the way they define the environmental debate by applying the analysis set out in Ellen Meiksins Wood's *Democracy Against Capitalism: Renewing Historical Materialism* to the current difficulty in dealing with environmental issues.

Chapter Three attempts to historicize the sustainability debate at the end of modernity by comparing it to the usury debate at the beginning of modernity. If sustainability is considered to be a moral concept which attempts to re-integrate economic relations within wider social institutions, the call for a moral economy in the usury debate provides an evocative basis for the consideration of the deep historicity of economy/society relations.

Chapter Four examines the dislocation of social relations which occur in the context of the imposition of capitalist relations in pumping surplus labour out of humans. By using the psychological categories of hysteria and paranoia to illustrate the way we "care" for the environment, it is my intention to point out that current environmental security considerations have more to do with protecting national security and economic interests, than with solving environmental problems.

Chapter Five provides a brief history of the relationship between capitalism and environmental policy making, especially in terms of how the public/private basis of capitalism confirms the separation of human history and natural history, where nature is the storehouse which supports economic imperatives.

Chapter Six and Seven are case studies in environmental policy making which illustrate the general points made in the earlier chapters. Chapter Six examines the case study of the Pacific salmon dispute between Canada and the United States, while Chapter Seven examines the failed attempt by the Canadian Government to develop endangered species protection legislation.

The Conclusion sets out what might be a viable approach to environmental policy associated with the expansion of the social realm, and this discussion is applied to environmental policy in the case of Canada's East Coast fishery, focusing on the creation of community-based conservation initiatives.

NOTES

1   Georg Simmel. 1990. *The Philosophy of Money*. David Frisby [Ed.]. New York: Routledge, p. 12.
2   I discuss this extensively in *The Oceans Are Emptying: Fish Wars and Sustainability*. Montreal: Black Rose Books, 1995.
3   Wolfgang Sachs. 1992. "Introduction." In *The Development Dictionary*. London: Zed Books, pp. 1–5.
4   Georg Lukács. 1971. "Reification and the Class Consciousness of the Proletariat." In *History and Class Consciousness: Studies in Marxist Dialectics*. [Trans. Rodney Livingstone]. London: Merlin Press, pp. 83–222.
5   Iain McGilchrist. 1995. "It's not so much thinking out what to do, it's the doing of it that sticks me." Review of Sass's book *Madness and Modernism* in *London Review of Books*, November 2, p. 29.
6   Jeffrey Simpson. 1997. "It's time Newfoundland took a brave stand on its fish industry," *Toronto Globe and Mail*, Sept. 18, A18.
7   Editor, *Toronto Globe and Mail*. 1997. "What farmers could teach the fishery." October 9, A18.
8   David Orr. 1994. *Earth in Mind: On Education, Environment, and the Human Prospect*. Washington: Island Press, p. 70.
9   Marshall Sahlins. 1985. *Islands of History*. Chicago: University of Chicago Press, p. vii.
10   Wolfgang Sachs. 1996. "Neo-Development: 'Global Ecological Management'." In *The Case Against the Global Economy and for a Turn to the Local*. Jerry Mander and Edward Goldsmith [Eds.]. San Francisco: Sierra Club Books, p. 240.
11   Colin Hay. 1994. "Environmental Security and State Legitimacy." In *Is Capitalism Sustainable? Political Economy and the Politics of Ecology*. Martin O'Connor [Ed.]. New York: Guilford, p. 217.
12   Hay. (1994:217).

13 Hay. (1994:218).
14 Ellen Meiksins Wood. 1995. *Democracy Against Capitalism: Renewing Historical Materialism.* New York: Cambridge University Press, p. 108
15 Meiksins Wood. (1995:275).
16 Sandor Ferenczi. 1955. *Final Contributions to the Problems and Methods of Psycho-analysis.* M. Balint [Ed.]. London: Hogarth Press and the Institute of Psychoanalysis, p. 66.
17 William Shakespeare. 1931. *King Lear.* Hardin Craig [Ed.]. New York: Scott, Foresman & Co. (III,vi,18.)
18 Val Plumwood. 1995. "Human Vulnerability and the Experience of Being Prey," *Quadrant*, March, pp. 29–24. Plumwood has also written a book entitled *Feminism and the Mastery of Nature.* (New York: Routledge, 1993).
19 Plumwood. (1995:34).
20 Norman O. Brown. 1959. *Life Against Death: The Psychoanalytical Meaning of History.* Middletown: Wesleyan University Press (1985 edition), p. 234–304.
21 W. H. Auden (from the poem "On the Waters He Walked" by Ralph Gustafson in *Visions Fugitive.* (Montreal: Véhicule Press, 1996).
22 Raymond Williams. 1980. "Ideas of Nature." In *Problems in Materialism and Culture.* New York: Verso, p.82.
23 Sahlins. (1985:ix–x).
24 Sahlins. (1985:xvii).
25 Sahlins. (1985:72).

II

The Trouble with Capitalism:
Environmental Concerns and the Privatization of
Political Power

[A]s a result of the whole UNCED process, the planet was
going to be worse off, not better ... We argue that UNCED
has boosted precisely the type of industrial development
that is destructive for the environment, the planet, and its
inhabitants. We see how, as a result of UNCED, the rich
will get richer, the poor poorer, while more and more of the
planet is destroyed in the process.

Pratrap Chatterjee and Matthias Finger[1]

After extensive involvement in the United Nations Commission on
Environment and Development negotiations leading up to the
"Earth Summit" in Rio de Janeiro in 1992, Chatterjee and Finger
arrive at the very dire assessment quoted above with regard to global
environmental policy making. My own personal experience with the all
but complete collapse of the fishery off the East Coast of Canada leads me
to a similar conclusion: as a result of resource management frameworks
established by the Canadian government to regulate the fishery, the rich
got richer, the poor poorer, and the marine biotic communities were exploited to the point of collapse in the process. What is required, then, in
terms of effective environmental policy is an understanding of current
economic relations which can account for this untenable situation. What
form of analysis can account for this kind of failure and point towards
initiatives that can overcome these failures?

It is my intention to link the failure of environmental policy with
the analysis of capitalism presented by Ellen Meiksins Wood in *Democracy Against Capitalism: Renewing Historical Materialism*.[2] Central to

Wood's analysis is the separation of the economic and political spheres, which she sees as defining to capitalism:

> The capitalist organization of production can be viewed as the outcome of a long process in which certain *political* powers were gradually transformed into *economic* powers and transferred to a separate sphere.[3]

Rooting out the buried social and political dimensions of the economy is the central project of environmentalism. This approach is based on the recognition that environmentalism is first and foremost a social and political struggle. The root causes have to do with relations based on appropriation and domination; and the main obstacles have to do with the movement of a wide array of political issues into the private sphere of expanding economic relations.

Attempts to find accommodations within capitalist relations for environmental concerns are failing on all sides, especially with regard to North-South relations, and nation-states are entirely incapable of promoting an environmental agenda, given their preoccupation with promoting the global economic agenda. A clear understanding of capitalism is required if it is to be challenged in the name of conservation of human communities and natural communities. This discussion necessarily has to deal with the relationship between human agency, historical specificity, and the logic of modes of production. If all we see in the emergence of capitalism is the working out of some essential human identity which has finally cast off the fetters of tradition and superstition, or a historical process which has finally emerged at its efficient and rational best, then all is lost with regard to ecological viability. As Wood states: "[the challenge is not to] assume the existence of capitalism in order to explain its coming into being ..."[4] As is evidenced in most analysis of economic globalization, the idea that, indeed, capitalism *has* a history remains scarcely acknowledged. Nowhere is this problem of understanding history more central than in trying to explain *historical change*, and nowhere is it more contentious than in explaining the emergence of capitalism. It is my intention to highlight the specificity of capitalism as a historical phenomenon, and to challenge the idea that there is anything developmental in history or human identity which would necessarily have us arrive at capital relations as some kind of "default position" at the "end" of history.

THE INVISIBLE COERCION OF CAPITALISM

> I am calling in question ... the notion that it is possible to describe a mode of production in economic terms, leaving aside as secondary (less 'real') the norms, the culture, the critical concepts around which this mode of production is organized.
>
> E. P. Thompson[5]

To engage in the practical project of challenging the historical forces of capitalism, it is necessary to account for this particular set of relations as arising out of qualitatively different sets of relations such as feudalism, without at the same time granting these processes an inevitability in historical terms, as if the nascent relations of capitalism incubated within those of feudalism. Focusing on the complex interrelations which generated the emergence of capitalism allows for a focus now on a concrete, experiential project of understanding current relations and processes, leading to a kind of kinetic relationality, rather than inertial materiality. A piece of paper is a ten-dollar bill only because we consent to participate in the relations that give it that authority.

Domination and exploitation are then to be seen as relationships and processes that gain visibility as they express themselves in terms of conflict, whether it is between an appropriating class and workers, or between Northern industrial interests and local Southern societies which provide resources for those industries. Conflict then becomes a useful basis upon which to engage in a historical inquiry because it is in conflict that a self-conscious conception of one's relations to the surrounding world become discussible.

The most aggressive basis for conflict currently — as it has been throughout most of modernity — is the requirements for capital to continue to expand. Capital can only do that now by ridding the world of any obstacles to the flow of resources, or capital, or of commodities to markets. It is this global agenda which is destroying whatever hope there might be for ecological viability. In the context of this conflict, what usually operates as the invisible coercion of capitalism becomes more visible and discussible; hence the insight, as stated earlier, which is provided to those who live in communities on the margins of this coercion.

What defines Western development is that it represents the earliest and most complete transfer of political power to private property, and the most thorough subservience of production to the demands of the appropriating *class*. In other historical periods, exploitation was carried out in terms of surplus extraction, but not necessarily in terms of controlling production. Capitalism is unique in its processes of domination and exploitation, because it is only in capitalism that the organization of production and of appropriation so completely coincide. It is also unique because it transforms struggles over appropriation into apparently non-political contests described in terms of economic rationality.[6]

In his discussion of relations in other historical periods, Robert Brenner states that: "... what distinguishes pre-capitalist property relations ... is that they provided the direct producers with the full means of reproduction."[7] In non-capitalist periods, surplus extraction was carried out by extra-economic forms of coercion such as aristocratic and religious authority, but left the forms of reproduction in place. What is significant about capitalism is that the extraction of surplus value is connected to the means of production through the extension of private property. With regard to the specificity of the particular appearance of capitalist relations in the countryside of Early Modern England as set out by Robert Brenner, Wood states that:

> ... the outcome [of the appearance of capitalism] was the subjugation of direct producers to the *imperatives* of competition, as they were *obliged* to enter the market for access to their means of subsistence and reproduction. At the heart of this account is the distinctive agrarian 'triad', the nexus of commercial landlord, capitalist tenant and wage-labourer which marked the most productive regions

in the English countryside ... Unlike the landlord or peas-
ant-proprietor, this English tenant has no secure rights of
property apart from the conditions of an economic lease,
and even his possession of land was subject to the requirements of a competitive market which compelled him
to increase productivity by innovation, specialization and
accumulation. The effect of these agrarian relations was to
set in train a new dynamic of self-sustaining growth with
no historical precedent.[8]

The intrusion of the market is precisely what has occurred in many Southern countries with regard to the promotion of such agendas as the so-
called "Green Revolution." The introduction of hybrid seeds, pesticides,
herbicides, and fertilizers results in local knowledge, local seeds, and local
markets being marginalized as the increasing "inputs" into agricultural
production purchased from large corporations requires massive increases
in "outputs" to support increased costs which are sold in global agricultural markets.[9] The minute the "expert" arrives in the farmyard with his bag
of wares, the farmer is rendered ignorant and dependent by the new forms
of knowledge and new industrial relations which inform farming practices.

In describing the specificity of the emergence of these new relations, it is Brenner's goal to "explain how historically specific conditions
produced capitalism's *unique* technological imperatives and its *unique*
expansionist drive."[10] This attempt to explain the specificity of the emergence of capitalism removes the idea of the "progressive directionality of
history," and is therefore at odds with the assumptions that exist in today's
world, where technological advance and economic expansion are universally taken for granted, as if they somehow emerge naturally out of the
earth. It is these forces of economy and technology which are many times
read back into the "progressive directionality of history" so as to explain
where we are now.

In taking up this project of examining the changes in social relations which produced capitalism, political theorists such as Wood and
Brenner are challenging the Enlightenment version of history in which
what was needed was not an explanation of a unique historical process

but simply an account of obstacles and their removal. Left on their own, self-interest guided by reason would produce capitalism, as if they only required the removal of what stood in their way, so that in modernity we could finally become who we are. The existence of capitalism, in other words, was assumed in order to explain its coming into being, as Wood argues. In the context of this representation of capitalist relations, globalization should therefore not appear as some kind of historical inevitability — driven as it is by these same forces of technological change and economic expansion — but instead as an intensification of appropriation and domination which, in turn, serve the requirements of the expansion of capital.

Driven by these expansionary forces, modern society becomes increasingly monocultural. As Marx states:

> The real barrier of capitalist production is capital itself. It is that capital and its self-expansion appear as the starting point and the closing point, the motive and the purpose of production; that production is only production for capital and not vice versa, the means of production are not mere means for the constant expansion of the living process of the society of producers.[11]

Nothing could be more important to worthwhile environmental action than the recognition that the definition of sustainability goals in terms "needs" (present needs versus future needs) is entirely insufficient to grapple with the fact that capitalism has nothing to do with needs. It has to do with the self-expansion of capital as the sole "motive" and "purpose" of production. That is all capital cares about. It abhors all communities but itself.

Injustice and exploitation are privileged and out of reach as they enter the domain wherein capital has entered into private relations with itself. This is what private means. Individuals have not developed a private internal reality (in psychoanalytic terms) so much as they have succumbed to the invasion into their being of the private economic interests. The idea that it is a private personal realm is a ruse, or at least if not a ruse, then a secondary refuge where what used to be social being now resides.

Those that operate within the domain of capital do so as embodied capital, doing the deeds of capital. Deadness has entered into private relations with itself.

THE SEPARATION OF THE "ECONOMIC" AND "POLITICAL" SPHERES

In order to get at the analytical failure which has accompanied ecological failure, it is useful to note what Wood considers to be a defining aspect of capitalism:

> ... there has been a tendency to perpetuate the rigid conceptual separation of the 'economic' and the 'political' which has served capitalist ideology so well ever since the classical economists discovered the 'economy' in the abstract and began emptying capitalism of its social and political content.[12]

Without challenging the separation of the political and economic aspects in capitalism, environmentalists will be continually confronted with the economic "explanations" for why things happen — its all so logical afterall — while at the same time a more limited conception of the political realm declares that these are issues that are beyond its jurisdiction.

The separation of the economic from the political — which is so taken for granted as a given and yet so specific to capitalism — provides capitalism with a very important defense mechanism against environmental resistance because economic concerns dominate while the political aspects of capitalism fade into the background, as in the false dichotomy of "jobs versus the environment." Central to addressing environmental problems is the recognition that environmental crisis is caused by the expansion of capital. For the most part, these problems have been "fobbed-off" as an issue to be dealt with either within the narrow realm of current public policy, or through increased efficiency of market mechanisms. Both of these approaches entirely fail to take in the buried social and political aspects of the economic exploitation of human communities and natural communities.[13]

For environmentalism to be successful, the internal workings of corporations have to be regarded as political domains, rather than economic ones, which are open for public debate, since these workings have such profound public consequences. Instead of this sort of challenge, there is the negotiation of the Multilateral Agreement on Investment (MAI), which strengthens the position of corporations and grants them the rights of citizens. What has happened in capitalism is that more and more political power has been siphoned off into the private economic sphere, rendering it beyond the reach of current democratic frameworks.

In order to understand the reasons for the separation of the economic from the political sphere, it is necessary to understand how and why capitalist relations came into existence, and the way they operate. Marx states that the starting point of capitalism "is nothing else than the historical process of divorcing the producer from the means of production."[14] What defines this divorce of the direct producer from the means of sustenance is the intervention of the state on behalf of those who are claiming control of that production. In order for the economy to come into existence as a separate sphere, political measures have to take place.

Hence the intervention of private interests into the public sphere carried out by the state — and the consequent loss of autonomy of those who formerly could sustain themselves — is at the very heart of capitalist relations. Capitalism is therefore a political set of relations masquerading as economic logic. The economy is a set of social relations, rather than market-driven forces. As Wood states:

> To ... insist on the social constitution of the economy is not at all to say that there *is* no economy, that there are no economic 'laws,' no mode of production, no 'laws of development in a mode of production, no law of capitalist accumulation, nor is it to deny that the mode of production is the 'most operative concept of historical materialism' ... It does not define production out of existence or extend its boundaries to embrace indiscriminately all social activi-

ties. It simply takes seriously the principle that a mode of production is a *social* phenomenon.

Equally important — and this is the point of the whole exercise — relations of production are, from this theoretical standpoint, presented in their political aspect, that aspect in which they are actually contested, as relations of domination, as rights of property, as the power to organize and govern production and appropriation. In other words, the object of this theoretical stance is a *practical* one, to illuminate the terrain of struggle by viewing modes of production not as abstract structures but as they actually confront people who must *act* in relation to them.[15]

Here is the "radical-practical" project of a transformative environmentalism: to see our current situation in its social and political dimensions, rather than in economic terms. By recognizing the political aspects of economic relations, opportunities for action appear. By contrast, to merely strategize with the various factors of late capitalism is to "mislead because they obscure not only the historical processes by which modes of production are constituted but also the structural definition of productive systems as living social phenomena."

Marx has been accused many times of being economically reductive and deterministic. But this criticism rest on the acceptance of the "economic" as a separate sphere from the wider realm of social relations, which then in turn defines those realms. This acceptance obscures the very division of the economic and political which Marx was trying to problematize by pointing out the specificity of relations in capitalism. For Marx, as Wood states:

> The 'sphere' of production is dominant not in the sense that it stands apart from and precedes these judicial-political forms, but rather in the sense that these forms are precisely forms of production, the *attributes* of a particular productive system ... [A] mode of production is not simply a technology but a social organization of productive

activity; and a mode of exploitation is a relationship of power.[16]

As it is currently conceived, public policy mechanisms are entirely insufficient in challenging these forces in their political aspect.

In order for the economy to become autonomous from other spheres of society, two things have to happen: first, the direct producer has to be separated from his or her livelihood; and second, the new conditions of work have to become the private concern of the appropriator so that a surplus can be generated from the labour of the formerly independent direct producer, which, in turn, serves as the "profit" in capitalism. Good business, then, is based on expropriation of the basis of survival so that a surplus can be extracted from the work of those who are consigned to sell their labour for less than it is worth. Such "good business" initiatives pervade calls for global competition, one of the end results of which is the appropriation of Southern resources. It is the politics of this situation which gets consigned to the realm of the autonomous economy:

> [The autonomy of the "economic" in capitalism is defined by relations where] surplus appropriation is achieved in ways determined by the complete separation of the producer from the conditions of labour and by the appropriator's absolute private property in the means of production ... In other words, the social allocation of resources and labour does not, on the whole, take place by means of political action, communal deliberation, hereditary duty, custom, or religious obligation, but rather through the mechanisms of commodity exchange.[17]

Commodity exchange creates an economic need in individuals, and this provides the compulsion which forces people to sell their surplus labour, as opposed to other historical periods where extra-economic forms of compulsion were used. The compulsion under capitalism only appears to be non-political because of the apparent separation of the economic and political spheres. Whereas in the past, power may have been political, judicial or religious, in capitalism it is economic pressure over those who are "free" from political, judicial or religious control. Hence, the invisible coercion of capitalism, and the profound difficulty of challenging it from the environmental perspective.

I have described the regulatory frameworks which have overseen the exploitation of fish on Canada's East Coast as an enclosure movement which generates depletion and dependence. The political arm of capitalism privatizes processes of meeting basic needs so that certain groups can garner profits from those it has expropriated. It is this process which explains the chronic inequality and over-exploitation in the fishery; a process which repeats itself again and again across the South in the context of globalization.

The separation of the economic and political — the burying of significant political aspects of appropriation within private spheres — hides a major political realm which has to do with environmental problems, and conversely, serves up a political jurisdiction which is significantly reduced in its mandate to regulate the forces of exploitation.

Just as privatization of government jurisdiction is a devolution of public power hitherto exercised by the state, so private property is an earlier version of devolution of state power to individuals or corporations from what had been a public domain. The linking of private property and the intensification of economic and technological exploitation — the benefits of which accrued into private hands — has driven the reason and the means of exploitation of human communities and natural communities.

It is not to say that all previous historical epochs were without their inequalities, but the particular relations of capitalism have allowed for the intensification of these forces of exploitation:

> Not only is the forfeit of surplus labour an immediate condition of production, but capitalist property unites to a degree probably not enjoyed by any previous appropriating class the power of surplus extraction and the capacity to organize and intensify production directly for the purposes of the appropriator. However exploitative earlier modes of production have been, however effective the

means of surplus extraction available to exploiting classes, in no other system has social production answered so immediately and universally to the demands of the exploiter.

At the same time, the powers of the appropriator no longer carry with them the obligation to perform social, public functions. In capitalism, there is a complete separation of private appropriation from public duties; and this means the development of a new sphere of power devoted completely to private rather than social purposes.[18]

Relating this analysis back to Chatterjee and Finger's claim that the rich get richer and the poor get poorer and the planet is degraded in the process, the poor are separated from their means of subsistence, and the rich are separated from public duties, and the private funneling of wealth takes no account of natural processes.

So not only is there a removal of direct access to the means of sustenance, there is also a withdrawal of the appropriators from having a public function which corresponds to the scale of private acquisition of benefits. Wood states:

The long historical process that ultimately issued in capitalism could be seen as an increasing — and uniquely well-developed — differentiation of *class* power as something distinct from *state* power, a power of surplus extraction not directly grounded in the coercive apparatus of the state. This would also be a process in which private appropriation is increasingly divorced from the performance of communal functions. If we are to understand the unique development of capitalism, then, we must understand how property and class relations, as well as the functions of surplus appropriation and distribution, so to speak, liberate themselves from — and yet are served by — the coercive institutions that constitute the state, and develop autonomously.[19]

The processes of appropriation and accumulation which remain unaccounted for when we accept the "rationality" of the economy explain why environmental problems are difficult to address. The ethical and moral aspects of the funneling of wealth on the one hand (and the exploitation of nature and humans that goes with it), and the abdication of collective responsibility on the other, are almost never discussed in the context of environmental issues. These realities remain firmly encased within the legality of late modern society. Indeed, these realities are being strengthened daily, despite the fact that it is poaching and black marketeering of the most invidious sort. We are legally destroying the world. Why is it so easy to institutionalize inequality and so difficult to institutionalize equality?

What this analysis of the evolution of capitalism points to is the recognition that the struggle against it requires a broad-based project:

> Struggles at the point of production ... remain incomplete as long as they do not extend to the locus of power on which capitalist property, with its control of production and appropriation, ultimately rests. At the same time, purely 'political' battles, over the power to govern and rule, remain unfinished until they implicate not only the institutions of the state but the political powers that have been privatized and transferred to the economic sphere. In this sense, the very differentiation of the economic and the political in capitalism ... is precisely what makes the unity of economic and political struggles essential ...[20]

The unity of the economic and political struggle challenges the game of musical chairs which is currently proceeding within the environmental policy process as the economic sphere expands and the public sphere shrinks, and the edicts of competitiveness come to dominate the failing concerns for the "public good." I want to emphasize here that the "political" is not synonymous with the nation-state, but rather, there is an important aspect of local control which constitutes political action in this context, as set out by initiatives such as community-based conservation, which offer viable possibilities for marginalized groups to begin to protect the natural communities on which they depend.

CAPITALISM AND ECONOMIC DEMOCRACY: CIVIL SOCIETY AND NEW SOCIAL MOVEMENTS

> Overcoming the privatization of political power may be even a central condition for the transformation of the labour process and the forces of production which is the distinguishing characteristic of capitalism.
>
> Ellen Meiksins Wood[21]

In order to engage in the practical issues of the struggle against domination and exploitation, it is necessary to understand how capitalism circumscribes current emancipatory debates as they relate to environmental concerns. In her discussion of current struggles against capitalism, Wood focuses on the multicultural debate in terms of the politics of identity and examines whether concepts such as "civil society" can provide an adequate political basis for challenging domination and exploitation. Wood's analysis of the multicultural debate and of civil society are instructive in setting out what might be considered an adequate political basis for environmental action. Wood states:

> At a time when a critique of capitalism is more urgent than ever, the dominant theoretical trends on the left are busy conceptualizing away the very idea of capitalism ... However diverse the methods of conceptually dissolving capitalism — including everything from the theory of post-fordism to post-modern 'cultural studies' and the 'politics of identity' — they often share one especially serviceable concept: 'civil society' ... However constructive this idea may be in defending human liberties against state oppression, or in marking out a terrain of social practices, institutions and relations neglected by the 'old' Marxist left, 'civil society' is now in danger of becoming an alibi for capitalism.[22]

Civil society may be able to challenge state oppression, but it may not be as effective in challenging economic oppression. What has become clear in the environmental movement is that every flag of protest that has been raised in defiance against the edicts of capitalism very quickly turns into a white flag of surrender, bleached out almost instantly by the "totalizing" power of capital. In the attempt to accommodate powerful interests and appear as rational professionals, environmentalists have willingly duped themselves into "becoming an alibi for capitalism." One of the central issues here is whether it is possible to establish a viable basis for environmental concerns within the context of capitalism.

Civil society requires as preconditions the existence of the state on the one hand, and the autonomous economy on the other. In other words, civil society arises out of a central aspect of capitalism and establishes its basis on one of the main ideological bulwarks, while doing so in the name of inclusiveness and participation. The advocates of civil society are strengthening our defense of non-state institutions and relations against the power of the state by tending to weaken our resistance to the coercion of capitalism through the acceptance of buried politics within the economic sphere.

What is missed many times, therefore, in discussions of non-governmental organizations (NGOs) is that trans-national corporations are NGOs and part of civil society. This occurs because discussions of NGOs take place in contrast to governments, and fail to include this economic aspect of civil society. Therefore the contrast between coercion, as embodied in the state, and freedom or voluntary action within civil society, is fallacious. When coercion was based on overt political power exercised by the state — as it was in earlier historical periods or is currently in China — the idea of civil society has an emancipatory capability. But this capability becomes more problematic when the political state becomes more benign — as it currently is in many industrialized countries — and the coercion arises from economic relations which can, in turn, be seen as synonymous with civil society. Wood states:

> Here, the danger lies in the fact that the totalizing logic and coercive power of capitalism becomes invisible, where the

> whole social system of capitalism is reduced to one set of
> institutions and relations among many others, on a con-
> ceptual par with households or voluntary associations.
> Such a reduction is, in fact, the principal distinctive feature
> of 'civil society' in its new incarnation. Its effect is to con-
> ceptualize away the problem of capitalism, by desegregat-
> ing society into fragments, with no overarching power
> structure, no totalizing unity, no systemic coercions — in
> other words, no capitalist system, with its expansionary drive
> and its capacity to penetrate every aspect of social life.[23]

Like the enlightened approach to the rational environmental policy process, civil society tends to presume that it can occupy a viable space
within capitalism, where it can go about its business without acknowledg-
ing that the results of these actions are circumscribed on all sides by
domination and exploitation.

In this context, it is possible to see the idea of civil society as one
that buries, rather than highlights, the forces of domination and exploitation, precisely because it requires the separation of the economic and
political in order to come into existence. At the same time, it borrows the
spurious rationality which is the inheritance of the economic sphere:

> One way of characterizing the specificity of 'civil society'
> as a particular social form unique to the modern world ... is
> to say that it constituted a new form of social power, in
> which many coercive functions that once belonged to the
> state were relocated in the 'private' sphere, in private prop-
> erty, class exploitation, and market imperatives. It is, in a
> sense, this 'privatization' of public power that has created
> the historically novel realm of 'civil society' ... [Civil soci-
> ety] represents a particular network of social relations which
> does not simply stand in opposition to the coercive, 'po-
> licing' and 'administrative' functions of the state but rep-
> resents the relocation of these functions, or at least a
> significant part of them ... by means of a thoroughly con-

centrated power of enforcement than has ever existed before.[24]

It is therefore exceedingly problematic to think of civil society as sphere of freedom and voluntary action without recognizing that the realm of the economic is the site of coercion. State and civil society relations represent the political and economic aspects of capitalism. Conceptions of civil society as a free space outside the coercive power of the state short-circuits the significance of economic relations as the site of oppression.

Although this new call for diversity in the multicultural debate may appear to go beyond former calls for tolerance, it is seriously undermined when it attempts to link "respect for difference" with economic issues:

> ... it is not at all clear that the new pluralism ... gets much beyond a statement of general principles and good intentions ... The new pluralism aspires to a democratic community which acknowledges all kinds of difference, of gender, culture, sexuality, which encourages and celebrates these differences, but without allowing them to become relations of domination or oppression ... But the 'politics of identity' reveals its limitations, both theoretical and political, the moment we try to situate *class* differences within its democratic vision ... The 'difference' that constitutes class as an identity *is*, by definition, a relationship of inequality and power, in a way that sexual or cultural difference need not be. A truly democratic society can celebrate diversities of life styles, culture, or sexual preference; but in what way would it be democratic to celebrate *class* differences?[25]

If equality is set out in terms of rights and equality which can be satisfied by legal and political principles, the question arises concerning whether it is possible to settle race and gender issues without having to deal with class issues. For example, in non-capitalist societies where inequality is based on judicial and political power rather than economic power, it would not be possible to separate race, class and gender issues, but in capitalist society, where there is so much political power buried in the economy, it is possible to separate class concerns from race and gender concerns. It is these formal equalities which tends to satisfy those interested in difference, and since there is still room for recognition of these differences in formal terms in capitalism without necessarily challenging it, class may have less in common with race and gender than first appears. Class is not an identity, it is an aspect of a whole social system. It is therefore impossible to promote emancipation based on class without challenging the systemic aspects of capitalism.

The same can be argued in environmental terms. The natural world is increasingly integrated into the logic of capitalism. It is not possible to promote ecological viability and species diversity within capitalism. It is necessary to alter the capitalist system in order to deal with environmental problems. In these terms, then, the ecological crisis is not a crisis of carrying capacity which requires increased efficiency and the internalization of costs, so much as it is a social crisis requiring a challenge to appropriation and domination.

ECONOMIC RATIONALITY AND ECOLOGICAL COLLAPSE

> The road to sustainable development passes through an undistorted, competitive, and all-encompassing market that gets the incentives right.
>
> Theodore Panayotou[26]

> To the extent that inter-regional dependency threatens geo-political security we have an argument for policies to enhance regional economic diversity, independence, and self-reliance, and to restrict trade to the exchange of real ecological surpluses. Needles to say, such prescriptions fly in the face of prevailing development rhetoric ...
>
> William Rees[27]

The range of opinion in the environmental debate is defined by the assumptions which are made about the role of the market in causing or ameliorating environmental problems. Those who accept the rationality of the market and see environmental problems as instances of market failure due to distortions caused by lack of property rights, or government subsidies or restrictions, therefore call for an expansion of the role of the market so that externalities can be properly internalized within the economic framework. Alternately, there is the recognition that over-exploitation of natural processes reflects the standard practice of capitalist relations, in which the market is only the outward face of a range of relations linked to appropriation and domination. What is defining here is the way in which the economic sphere is understood: those who accept it as a given and understand that it operates in a rational manner in "economic" terms; and those who see the economy as a site of buried "social and political" relations which is underwritten by interests and class differentiation.

In his book *Green Markets: The Economics of Sustainable Development*, Theodore Panayotou explains environmental problems in terms of situations where the market was not able to operate properly, and that the market provides the opportunity for connecting economic activity and ecological viability:

> The answers to these questions are found in the disassociation of scarcity and price, benefits and costs, rights and responsibilities, actions and consequences. This disassociation exists because of a combination of market and policy failures. The prevailing configuration of markets and policies leaves many resources outside the domain of markets, unowned, unpriced, and unaccounted for ... The result is an incentive structure that induces people to maximize their profits not by being efficient and innovative but by appropriating other people's resources and shifting their costs onto others.[28]

What is interesting here is that whereas Wood sees this appropriation as central to domination in capitalism, Panayotou sees appropriation as an example of market failure within capitalism, of capitalism not working properly, whether it is due to "market failure [caused by] failures arising from unpriced or open-access resources, insecure tenure, and ... high transaction costs" or "policy failure ... defined as government intervention that distorts a well-functioning market."[29] These failures prevent prices from rising in line with "growing scarcities" and "rising social costs" which would "restore the balance between supply and demand." Solving environmental problems, therefore, involves expanding the role of the market:

> It is a misconception, therefore, that the presence of market failures justifies a reduction in the role of the market in resource allocation and an increase in the role of government. To the contrary, mitigation of market failures through secure property rights, internalization of externalities, increased competition, and reduced uncertainty would enhance the role of markets in allocating resources such as water, land, fisheries, forests, and environmental services and would make it unnecessary to establish cumbersome and often inefficient public institutions for resource management and conservation. The government need only provide the initial institutional and policy reform necessary to allow the markets to function efficiently.[30]

Panayotou's main focus is North-South relations, and he calls for the very things that, in Wood's analysis, will intensify appropriation and domination by draining the market of its politics, and presenting its operation as rational and efficient, where "... the acid test of successful policy interventions is the elimination of policy-induced market distortions,"[31] and where sustainability is achieved through "... the substitution of human capital for natural resources."[32]

As is clear in his use of such terms as "human capital" and "natural resources," Panayotou is untroubled by the social and political aspects of the market, and the pumping of surplus labour out of humans and surplus resources out of nature. It is worthwhile to contrast Panayotou's belief that a properly functioning market creates conditions for ecological viability, with William Rees' contention, in his essay "Pressing Global Limits: Trade as the Appropriation of Carrying Capacity," that the "default position" of most economists and politicians today is a belief in the benefits of global free trade. In contrast to Panayotou, Rees sets out a conception of free trade "which fly[s] in the face of current development rhetoric" by highlighting the intensification of inequity between Northern and Southern countries when exploitation of Southern resources serve Northern industrial interests.

It is possible to link Wood's analysis of appropriation and domination with what Rees describes as the appropriation of the carrying capacity of the South by the North. In more specific historical terms, the expansionary nature of capitalism is currently expressing itself in terms of economic globalization whereby the North gains freer access to the resources and labour of the South. As Wood states with regard to the necessary conditions for the emergence and expansion of capitalism and the relations of domination which are generated:

> The evolution of an economic system in which all production is subordinated to the self-expansion of capital, to the imperatives of accumulation, competition and profit maximization, required something more than the simple growth of markets and the traditional practices of buying cheap and selling dear. It even required something more than widespread production for exchange. The very specific integration of production and exchange entailed by this system — in which the economy is driven by competition and profit is determined by improving labour productivity — presupposed a transformation of social property relations which subjected direct producers to market imperatives in historically unprecedented ways, by making their very access to the means of subsistence and self-reproduction market dependent.[33]

Rees conveys this process of appropriation in similar terms:

> ... to the extent that trade and the restructuring of rural economies displace people from productive landscapes to

> overcrowded cities, particularly in the South, to supply urban industrial regions, mainly in the North, they contribute to impoverishment, urban migration, and local ecological decay. Moreover, to the extent that the current international development model favours the net transfers of wealth to the North and the depletion of natural capital in the South, this poverty and ecological decline is a chronic condition. The people of less developed countries cannot live simultaneously on carrying capacity exported to the world's industrial heartlands.[34]

It is this "chronic condition" which is not only associated with the "current international development model" but with the expanding relations of capitalism over the last four hundred years.

Rees argues that, as opposed to the standard idea in economics that trade overcomes local constraints and that carrying capacity is infinitely expandable:

> … any perceived increase in carrying capacity is illusion. In fact, by enabling all regions to exceed local limits simultaneously … and by exposing regional ecological surpluses to global demand, unregulated international trade eventually reduces global carrying capacity, accelerating the encroachment of limits and increasing the risk of ecological collapse to all.[35]

This untenable situation is generated when "industrialized countries 'appropriate' a disproportionate share of global carrying capacity, much of it through commercial trade, effectively preempting developing economies from using their fair share."[36]

In her analysis of Latin American societies throughout the Colonial period, Elinor Melville conveys this process of appropriation in terms of the evolution of a global division of labour where former colonies produce resources for use by the industrial centre.[37] Melville sets out a genesis of economic relations which has created the current realities of inequity and over-exploitation in this way:

... as the international system of [colonial] exchange grew, relations between states became increasingly shaped by considerations of international trade. But then something occurred in one specific region of this global system that transformed the international order: the replacement of animate with inanimate energy and thus the theoretical possibility of infinite increase in the production of manufactured goods ... transforming it into a system of production as well as exchange.[38]

The amalgamation of a system of exchange with a system of production transformed colonial dependency into a dependency based on resource output in industrial markets:

... industrialization developed within the context of an international system of exchange; and all the changes associated with industrialization, such as the appearance of capitalist relations of production, formation of nation states etc., fanned out through the system. The result was the transformation of a system of exchange between producing regions, into a system of distribution that sustained production in one part of the exchange network.[39]

With regard to environmental concerns, Melville comes to the same conclusion as Rees in terms of the causes of inequity and over-exploitation related to the politics of the market:

As region after region of the former colonial system has been locked into the global system of production by debt, they have lost their autonomy of development and have instead become both the dependents and the support of the industrial regions. And, as they struggle to sustain both their own development and that of the industrial regions, they become even more underdeveloped and even more likely to practice "unsustainable" methods of extraction of raw materials needed to sustain the centre. That they have little choice in the matter is the result of the developmental process of the world-order itself.[40]

This could just as well be a description of the history of Canada's East Coast fishery.

The politics of this situation leads to a form of appropriation that is generated by unequal power relationships between economic interests in the North, and Southern countries. As well, this process of appropriation of local production by powerful economic interests, and the corresponding lack of political leverage to challenge this appropriation, is central to the ecological plight we currently face in global terms. This conception of appropriation and domination can also serve for a precise definition of capitalism. The ecological crisis and the relationships which inform that crisis are directly connected to the very structures and processes of capitalism.

NOTES

1   Pratrap Chatterjee and Matthias Finger. 1994. *The Earth Brokers: Power, Politics and World Development*. New York: Routledge, pp. 2–3.
2   Ellen Meiksins Wood. 1995. *Democracy Against Capitalism: Renewing Historical Materialism*. New York: Cambridge University Press.
3   Meiksins Wood. (1995:36).
4   Meiksins Wood. (1995:117).
5   E. P. Thompson. 1978. "Folklore, Anthropology, and Social History," *Indian Historical Review*, 3 (2), pp. 17–18.
6   Meiksins Wood. (1995:44).
7   Robert Brenner. 1989. "Bourgeois Revolution and Transition to Capitalism." In *The First Modern Society*. A. L. Beier et al. [Eds.]. New York: Cambridge University Press, p. 287.
8   Ellen Meiksins Wood. 1991. *The Pristine Culture of Capitalism*. New York: Verso, pp. 10–11.
9   Vandana Shiva. 1993. *Monocultures of the Mind: Perspectives on Biodiversity and Biotechnology*. London: Zed Books.
10   Meiksins Wood. (1995:119–20).
11   Karl Marx. 1971. *Capital* III. Moscow: International Publishers, p. 250.
12   Meiksins Wood. (1995:19).

13   Colin Hay. 1994. "Environmental Security and State Legitimacy." In *Is Capitalism Sustainable? Political Economy and the Politics of Ecology* Martin O'Connor [Ed.]. New York: Guilford, pp. 217–31.

14   Karl Marx. 1971. *Capital*. Moscow: International Publishers, p. 668.

15   Meiksins Wood. (1995:25).

16   Meiksins Wood. (1995:27).

17   Meiksins Wood. (1995:28–29).

18   Meiksins Wood. (1995:31).

19   Meiksins Wood. (1995:31).

20   Meiksins Wood. (1995:47).

21   Meiksins Wood. (1995:40).

22   Meiksins Wood. (1995:238).

23   Meiksins Wood. (1995:245).

24   Meiksins Wood. (1995:254).

25   Meiksins Wood. (1995:258).

26   Theodore Panayotou. 1993. *Green Markets: The Economics of Sustainable Development*. San Francisco: Institute for Contemporary Studies Press, p. 144.

27   William E. Rees. 1994. "Pressing Global Limits: Trade as the Appropriation of Carrying Capacity." In *Growth, Trade and Environmental Values*. Ted Schrecker and Jean Dalgleish [Eds.]. London, Ont.: Westminster Institute, p.48.

28   Panayotou. (1993:26).

29   Panayotou. (1993:27).

30   Panayotou. (1993:30).

31   Panayotou. (1993:31).

32   Panayotou. (1993:141).

33   Meiksins Wood. (1995:157).

34   Rees. (1994:45).

35   Rees. (1994:29–30).

36   Rees. (1994:30).

37   Elinor Melville. 1994. "Underdevelopment and Unsustainability in Historical Perspective." In *Human Society and the Natural World*. David V.J. Bell, Roger Keil, and Gerda Wekerle [Eds.]. York University: Faculty of Environmental Studies, pp. 14–19.

38   Melville. (1994:15–16).

39   Melville. (1994:16).

40   Melville. (1994:17).

III

The Call for a Moral Economy:
The Usury Debate and the Sustainability Debate

Usury is ... the deceiving of the brethren ... works of darkness ... a monster in nature ... plague of the world ... misery of the people ... a theft which continues day and night without ceasing ... [and feeds on] the hunger of others.

Norman Jones[1]

R. H. Tawney argued that to study the economy without exploring the wider institutional context in which it exists is like a geographer discussing river systems without mentioning mountains. Contrary to Tawney's advice, it has been more popular recently for politicians and economists to emphasize the "invisible hand" of the market — as if it were some self-sustaining, propagating mechanism — rather than the more visible social institutions and citizen consent which make market economy possible. This lends an evangelical and naive tone to a great deal of economic discussion, as it focuses on an autonomous economy evolving on its own terms, and leading John Cassidy to describe economics as "an obtuse discipline that often appears to resemble a branch of mathematics."[2] This enclosed approach to economics leads to a sense of inevitability in the expansion of markets in modern society, and ignores the fact that this evolution was a self-conscious process created by interests and groups at every stage.

In comparing the usury debate (1571–1624) and the sustainability debate, I am attempting to move discussion from the internally "rational" economic framework to the wider societal context, and in doing so, ask the question: Is environmentalism engaging in a project that sufficiently challenges the increasing autonomy of market economy in a way that re-establishes the primacy of relations in human communities and natural communities? It is generally accepted that sustainability is first and fore-

53

most a moral initiative having to do — in its weakest definitions — with inter-generational equity (meeting the needs of present generations without compromising the ability of future generations to meet their needs), and in its strongest terms, sustainability is associated with North-South equity concerns, as well as equity of members within societies, who have unequal access to the market.

Tawney set out the analytical challenge at the beginning of modernity with regard to usury in these terms: "What requires explanation is not the view that these [economic] matters are the province of religion, but the view that they are not."[3] At the "end" of modernity, what requires explanation is not whether the relationship between environment and economy are the province of society generally ("What is the purpose of society, anyway?"), but the view that they are not. The usury debate (usury defined as a "loan with a contract for interest") therefore is an especially evocative point of comparison for current environmental reform because both are concerned with the relationship between economics and societal institutions.

The usury debate at the beginning of modernity marks the controversial movement of economics from being inseparable from social and religious institutions, to gradually having an increasingly autonomous role defined by its own terms, at the same time as granting power to groups who benefited from this increased autonomy. A recognition of how anomalous this autonomy is in historical terms is central to a clear understanding of environmental challenges. The environmental debate at the end of modernity attempts to re-integrate economics into wider societal institutions through concepts such as sustainability. As Michael Jacobs states in *The Green Economy: Environment, Sustainable Development and the Politics of the Future*:

> ... sustainability is an *ethical* concept. To the orthodox economist this is a criticism; indeed, it places sustainability outside the realm of economics ... any policy decision on the environment will involve an ethical choice.[4]

This ethical basis for sustainability removes it from the autonomous workings of the economy and makes it the concern of those who see the goal of the economy as equitably serving present needs, as well as the projected needs of future generations. As Jacobs states: "If we are concerned about the interests of future generations, we must also surely be concerned about people living in poverty today."[5]

It is instructive for any current discussion which now attempts to re-integrate economics with a wider set of environmental and social values at the end of modernity to recognize that there was an intense, half-century-long debate which finally allowed for the initial separation of economics from social institutions at the beginning of modernity. The contrasting assumptions which inform these two historical debates separated by 400 years can give some idea of the transformations which have occurred in modernity and can underscore the challenge of finding ethical solutions to environmental problems.

What is abundantly clear in comparing the usury debate and the sustainability debate is the deep historicity which underwrites the relationship between economy and society. This deep historicity is a central challenge to those who attempt to transform unsustainable structures and processes into sustainable ones. The bringing together of these two debates also problematizes the progressive conception of modernity in which rationality triumphs over superstition and religion. The undue optimism of the Whig version of history is severely circumscribed by the fact that at the end of modernity there is an attempt to relocate this emergent economic rationality within moral concepts such as sustainability so as to avoid what appears to be a grim future for the biosphere.

In his book *God and the Moneylenders*, Norman Jones recounts the triumph of particular conditions which have come to be associated with modernity: the creation of the individual and the dominance of rational economic thinking. In the evolution of points of view about the law against usury, the increasing emphasis in some theological circles on internal conscience as the guide to a Christian life, and the vast economic changes of the period related to the emergence of agricultural and merchant capitalism combined unintentionally to relegate the ethics of economic relationships to be a marginal consideration in social terms. When that happened, economic expediency was left as the only sure way for society to judge when usury occurred and whether it was good or bad.[6]

The "realm of the conscience" and "economic expediency" present the twin processes of the internalization of meaning in individual conscious-ness and the free rein of economics in the world. Garrett Hardin argues that conscience is "self-eliminating" in the communityless, cultureless tragedy of the commons, and what we see in the usury debate is the nascent retreat of God and morality from the social world that would allow for Hardin's metaphor to come into being.

If the current realities of globalization reflect a world in which capi-tal abhors all communities but itself, the prohibition against usury at the beginning of modernity reflects a situation where social and religious community abhors capital. In other words, whereas the priorities of glo-balization defines a world from within an increasingly pervasive economic logic, usury presents an ethical and religious view of capital almost en-tirely "from without" economics. This, then, creates an alternate pole from which to view the working of modern economy which has a basis in the history of Northern countries. It is this alternate pole "from without" eco-nomics which can also be connected to local Southern cultures who are struggling to maintain their social relations of "moral economy" in the midst of the expansion of Northern economic interests.[7]

THE THEOLOGY OF USURY

Jones sets the usury debate which occurred in 16th and 17th century England in the context of the increasingly dominant role modern economy was beginning to play in English society at the time. Jones states:

> This is the biography of the Act Against Usury of 1571. It
> seeks to understand the birth, life, and death of the statute
> by placing it into the intellectual, legal, economic, and so-
> cial contexts that created it, gave it meaning and killed it in
> 1624.[8]

In describing the transformations which bracketed this life and death, Jones argues that whereas the debate that created the act which prohib-ited usury in 1571 was dominated by "scholastic modes of analysis and questions about God's will," the 1624 act which repealed the act treated usury "as an economic matter" and "ignored God, except for a peculiar amendment that insisted that the Act did not repeal the law of God in conscience."[9]

In order to set out what it is that is being prohibited in the laws against usury, Jones defines usury as:

> ... a contract intentionally for more than the principle of a loan without risk to the lender. Usury occurred only when the lender was guaranteed a profit without regard to the borrower's risk. Usury is a loan with a contract for interest.[10]

In this prohibition, the viability of ethical and religious community is paramount, and there is a clear recognition that economic relations are subject to ethical and religious values, and that "a loan with a contract for interest" is destructive to those values.

In the 16th century, a great deal of the usury debate rested on the work of theologian Thomas Aquinas. Aquinas began his discussion of usury by setting out the difference between fungibles, which were consumed by their use, and non-fungibles, which were not destroyed by their use. A fungible good cannot be rented or leased because it cannot be returned intact to its owner. Thus one cannot rent food. By contrast, a non-fungible, such as a house, can be leased or rented because it is not destroyed by its use.

Aquinas described money as a fungible, in which case ownership and use are identical. In the same way that the loan of food is useless unless one can eat it (and therefore interest could not be charged), paying interest on money lent is to pay twice for one thing, or to require payment for something that does not exist. A money loan must, because of money's fungible nature, be a sale of money, for which repayment is full compensation. To charge for the use of the money as well as for the sale — to demand payment with interest — is, therefore, Aquinas argued, a form of fraud. If you use money, you no longer have the use of it; therefore to pay for the use is to pay rent on something you do not have, and which cannot be returned to the original owner. Therefore interest on a loan is a form of theft, and theft is a sin.

This kind of argument does not, of course, readily apply to the pervasive interest-bearing reality of the late-20th century, where it is possible to use money without destroying it through investments. In fact, part of the problem in the relations between economics and the environment is that economics views the world as non-fungible, where carrying capacity is infinitely expandable, whereas from the environmental point of view, economic relations are eating the fungible world and charging interest in the process.

The Medieval approach to usury was not applied universally, but instead allowed for some inconsistencies with regard to lenders who might suffer a loss if the borrower was delinquent in repaying, or if the lender suffered from lost opportunities by not having the use of the money while it was lent. This, in turn, led to allowance for interest being charged (what an economist might call lost "opportunity cost," as if within the self-expansion of capital, time becomes a continuous opportunity to invest).

These inconsistencies gradually expanded because of changing economic circumstances in 15th century England, which in turn generated different forms of analysis of the ideas concerned with usury. As the opportunities for productive employment of capital increased, moralists were led to judge the justifications for profit differently. Financial risk as a justification for charging interest, along with a greater willingness to accept the social utility of financiers, led to a wider acceptance of interest-bearing loans which began to make room for large-scale commercial transactions.

Despite these inconsistencies, the usury debate took place in close proximity to the relations between humanity, God, and law. Broadly speaking, there were two distinct positions on usury in Early Modern England: the "objectivist," Aquinian position enshrined the law that lending at interest was always wrong, with few exceptions; and the "subjective" nominalist position which acceded to the Aquinian definition, but refused to accept any external objective measurement of the crime. For some Protestants such as Calvin, there was a new-found emphasis on individual intentions, rather than external actions, whereby "God would judge the secrets of the lender's heart."[11]

Commentators such as John Jewel upheld the Aquinian position by arguing that even with borrowing between the rich, someone is made hungry because someone has to pay the interest, someone has to sell the surplus value of their labour to create the wealth for the rich man. Wealth is not an innocent act. Thereby, "The civil law condemneth it, the canon law condemneth it, the temporal law condemneth it, and the law of nature condemneth it."[12]

The censure of usury originated in the ethic of not making money on a borrower's need (the golden rule). But when circulation of money became increasingly the norm, the borrower wanted the loan not out of need, but for profitable investment. The argument was that "whenever the money goes out of your hands there is a cessation of gain, and thus it is proper that you be reimbursed for your loss."[13]

Therefore the ethic in maintaining civil or religious society was challenged by the context of profit ("gain"), and the censure against usury was eclipsed by changing economic realities, transformed from tribal brotherhood to universal otherhood, as Benjamin Nelson claims.[14] Compensating individual lenders for the "cessation of gain" was beginning to rival the primacy of religious community.

Alternately, those who were in favour of relaxing the laws of usury in Early Modern England argued in terms of charity and equity: to the stark beggar give freely, to the poor householder lend freely, and to the rich merchant "when dealing with one who would use the money to make a profit the lender has a right to share in the gain" and "Hope of gayne maketh men industrious, and where no gayne ys to bee had, men will not take paynes."[15]

The pragmatic side of the usury debate therefore argued that if lender and borrower were in charity with one another, there was no usury, and since these attitudes could not be decided legally, it freed lenders and borrowers to follow their consciences, knowing that God would take care of the moral realm, whereas the state should regulate in the secular interest of the common good.

In other words, if it is possible to compare the religious conservatives in the usury debate with the economic globalizers in the sustainability debate, we have gone from living within community in the usury debate where the world is understood entirely in community terms, to living off the "interest" produced by nature in the sustainability debate where the world is entirely understood in terms of productive capacity. This transition is a graphic metaphor for the way society has been transformed by market economy.

The increasingly contentious relationship between religious law and economic logic formed the basis of the usury debate which began in the British parliament in 1571. Although there was great disagreement on usury, there was one issue that concerned everyone: the deleterious effects usury had on the social hierarchy. There was general agreement that unchecked usury inverts the social order by making the world the Devil's so that people no longer know their place. For those concerned with the usury debate, political economy and moral economy were synonymous with God's economy, but the differences arose in conceptions of the relationship between God and society. This difference in theological approach related to different concepts of the relationship between God's law and secular law, and the role personal conscience played in that relationship, and the larger question of the way changing economic relations were individualizing and internalizing bases of understanding in what had been a generalized religious sense of community. As Wood has set out, society is moving from extra-economic forms of surplus extraction based on hierarchy and tradition to the invisible coercion of money that grows.

THE EVOLUTION OF USURY LAW 1571–1624: CHANGING ASSUMPTIONS ABOUT SALVATION

A bastard child borne, usury is taken now to be almost legitimate.

Henry Rowlands[16]

The debate over the creation of the usury law of 1571 revolved around theological questions about what constitutes usury and what should be done about it. The conservative followers of Aquinas believed that usury was always wrong and was condemned by God, whereas the revisionists believed that usury was wrong if it breached the rule of equity and charity, while the pragmatists believed that it was necessary to be realistic and to operate within English law. As a series of compromises, the Act Against Usury of 1571 still regarded usury as evil, although it allowed for more liberal exceptions to the rule.

The conservative arguments has to do with the ideas that usury promoted covetousness, and was detrimental to society. The collection of interest would allow people to stop working as they lent their money out at the highest of rates. This competition for money would also tend to exclude the poor who could not pay the high rates of interest. And in general, the conservatives believed the wholesale pursuit of wealth would undermine a divinely ordained social structure whereby the usurer would "gnawth and teareth out his gaine, out of the hands and lively-hoodes not onely of the commonalty, but gentry, yea nobility of this land."[17]

Jones outlines the view of the world upon which the censures against usury were based, and which was under threat by new historical realities in the late-16th century, and reflecting conflict between extra-economic and economic coercion:

> First, they assumed that relationships were largely customary. A person had a place in communal society, and was bound by custom to perform certain duties. There was no agreement or choice in performing them. Frequently reinforced by law, customary relationships were seldom distinguished from moral obligations. Then, too, a producer's relationship to craft and customers tended to be customary. The work done, the way it was done, how it was sold, and the price charged were regulated by custom and law. Second, economic ideas and ethical ideas were closely linked, and economic freedom was constrained by ethical considerations. People were not free to do as they chose, not even with their property, and economic relations were subject to considerations of morality and station. Property and wealth were gifts from God to be used as He required. Third, a person had freedom of choice only within the limitations imposed by duty to God and neighbours. These

assumptions led to the expectation that the laws governing human relationships should ensure fairness and jus-
tice in economic relations.[18]

From the Protestant perspective at the time, there is a gradual shift in
discussions of usury away from the primacy of custom outlined above.
Gone are the discussions of "unnatural acts," and there is more of an
emphasis on Christian equity. By the 1590s, there begins to be a recognition that usury is a matter of internal conscience and that paying usurious
rates was not always sinful. This transition was made room for by the
general movement from a focus on religious community towards the primacy of the individual's conscience guided by God. Commentators such
as Roger Fenton decried the increasing primacy of the role of individual
conscience, as opposed to the more collective sense of devotion and
practice which had focused on "good works":

> For every mans Quaere is not ... 'What shall we doe?' but
> what shall we thinke? Whereas cases of conscience, doe
> sleepe with conscience, which of all questions are the most
> profitable, and least regarded: so loth are men to restraine
> affection, and limit their actions. Yet of all such cases this
> of usurie hath most need to be revived. For in this, the
> custome of sinning doth not onlely take away the sense,
> but the acknowledgment of sinne ...[19]

This movement from works to thoughts indicates a contraction of the
social sphere and individual identity which are essential to understanding
the long-term significance of the expansion of economic activity. Arguments about the necessity of economic activity replace "good works" in
the world, and conscience becomes a temporary way-station as these
social relations begin to disappear from the world, which, in turn, reflects
a displacement of attention away from participation in the world.

At this time there was also a shift from attention focused on how
and why usury is a sin to discussions about the importance of having a
contract with the borrower so that the lender can be protected because

the contract will make the debtor more careful to repay, preventing an unjust default on the loan, and discouraging the squandering of the loan, which is also a sin. What is evident in the transformation reflected in the usury debate is that economic activity is shifting from its intermittent role in terms of the distribution and consumption of goods that was linked to harvest time, to serving the increasingly demanding needs of more complex forms of production. Rather than production being a static given linked to agricultural output and traditional forms of surplus extraction, and economic activity concerned with the distribution of goods in local markets, emerging conceptions of the "culture of improvement" led to relations in production becoming a more defining aspect of social reality.

Walter Howse, in his "Treatise on Usury" (1605) outlined the profile of the new, lawful usurer, and it conveys the increasing internalization of conscience and the free rein of economics in the world. The good usurer:

1) lends not from greed, but from a modest desire for gain;
2) covenants for a certain gain, but is willing to remit in whole or in part if need be;
3) takes bills and bonds, but in soul is inwardly resolved to hazard the principle if the borrower loses it.
4) Though the borrower's gain from the loan is great, the lender will never charge more than the legal rate of interest.
5) The lender never takes biting interest of the rich or the poor;
6) often lends freely, without looking for the return of the loan;
7) is ready to forgive the debtor if the latter is in need, and to help in this need;
8) thanks God for all blessings;
9) takes no interest unless it is compatible with the common good.[20]

None of these elements are new in the usury debate, but what Howse had done differently is locate all of these elements in the conscience. As Jones states: "There, hidden from all, lies the factor that determines if a loan is sinful. On the outside one loan cannot be told from another ..." The logical end of these transformations in the usury debate is a religious rationale for capitalist behaviour. What followed was a reduction of usury to a matter of conscience and secular convenience. God would punish or reward the intentions of the heart, but human law could not. In the same way that the buried politics of the economy rendered itself beyond the realm of public policy, so the realm of conscience rendered inaccessible the ethical questions concerning community.

Instead, the state should concern itself with regulating loans in terms of the interests of society. This made lending at interest a secular economic activity with positive or negative effects on society, much like regulating monetary policy. By separating sin and behaviour, people were free to seek economic answers to exchange rather than debating their significance in terms of ethics and scripture. The arguments against usury tended now to have more to do with the deleterious effects high interest rates would have on trade and economic activity. The internalization of sin led to a redefining of the role of the state in more limited secular terms, since it could no longer regulate the relationship between individual conscience and God. Jones describes it in this way:

> By insisting that sin was an internal matter and by demanding that the individual be as free as possible to follow the dictates of God the theologians of this [Puritan] school separated the realm of the secular from the realm of the spiritual, depriving the terrestrial government of its right to enforce God's law and forcing it to turn to secular justifications for its actions. At the same time, by removing the centre of moral judgment from the community to the individual conscience they admitted that what each person intended by one's actions could only be judged by intention. This had the practical effect of freeing individual action ... By disconnecting intention from action they were freeing people to act in their own self-interest in a way unheard of in English theology ... The theologians had

cleared the way for the emergence of economics as a science separate from theology. In the process they had given the governing classes of England a new way to analyse laws which affected markets, money, and social behaviour.[21]

At the beginning of modernity, therefore, the separation of the sacred and the secular provided the basis for the creation of the separate spheres of the political and the economic, which are defining realities in the expansion of capitalist relations. Although these changes brought with them a sense of increased personal freedom and increased freedom of the state to make policy free of the edicts of God, what eventually became evident is that economic discipline became a more ruthless and vigilant controller of human behaviour than previous forms of surplus extraction. "[F]reeing individual action" from religious restrictions has a similar function to freeing the economy from the restrictions of public policy.

MORAL ECONOMY AND HISTORICAL TRANSFORMATION

At the same time as the increasing primacy of economic activity was reshaping the relationship between economy and society — as evidenced in the way that discussions of usury moved from the religious frame of reference to one of economic exigency — there were transformations in relationships between groups from ones based primarily on privilege and tradition to ones increasingly defined by trade and commerce. In this transition, there were many groups who lost their position in one world and had not as yet secured a new place in the unfolding of an emergent economic order. Christopher Hill's illustration of this period through the use of the term "masterless men" who increasingly inhabited common lands and expanding cities, reflects this dislocation.[22] As Tawney states with regard to this social and economic transformation:

> It was, indeed, the collision between the vested interests of the peasants and master craftsmen and new forms of capitalist enterprise which produced the social tension of the Tudor period ... where [to quote Harrison] "the ground

> of the parish is gotten up into a few men's hands, yea,
> sometimes into the tenure of one, or two, or three, whereby
> the rest are compelled either to be hired servants unto the
> other, or else to beg their bread in misery from door to
> door."[23]

What was clear to many at the beginning of modernity was that the "rationality" of economic relations which was being given freer rein in the world was also posing a serious threat to moral and religious conceptions of society. They did so by generating new forms of inequality in terms of appropriation of wealth and land into private hands what had in the past been considered to be part of the common weal of society. The ongoing debate on usury at the end of the 16th and beginning of 17th centuries reflects the movement of lending from being, to quote Tawney, "spasmodic, irregular, unorganized, a series of individual, and sometimes surreptitious, transactions"[24] based on mutual aid, to being more of a systematic specialty which had particular ramifications for the various groups in English society at the time:

> Unconscionable bargains are made at all times and in all
> places. What gave their particular significance to the trans-
> actions of the money lender in the sixteenth century was
> that they were not a mere incident on the frontiers of eco-
> nomic life, but touched the vital nerves of the whole social
> system ... The crucial matter is that of the relations of the
> producer to the dealer with whom he buys and sells, and to
> the small capitalist, often the dealer in another guise, to
> whom he runs into debt ... Almost everyone ... has need of
> the moneylender. And the lender is often a monopolist —
> "a money master," a maltster or corn monger, "a rich priest,"
> who is the solitary capitalist in a community of peasants
> and artisans. Naturally, he is apt to become their master.[25]

In response to the increasing recognition that there was a relationship between scarcity of corn supply leading to privation and the actions of merchants and speculators, rather than just to a bad harvest, there were a series of emergency measures that were taken to insure that people did not starve. These measures were codified during the same period as the usury debates (roughly 1580–1630) and were set out in what was called *The Book of Orders*. The emergency measures required that magistrates attend local markets,

> and where you shall fynde that there is insufficiente quantities broughte to fill and serve the said marketts and speciallie the poorer sorte, you shall thereupon resorte to the houses of the Farmers and others using tyllage ... and viewe what store and provision of graine they have remayninge either thrashed or unthrashed ...[26]

The Book of Orders therefore empowered magistrates to inventory the amount of corn in storage in a local area and to order sufficient quantities of that stock to be sent to the local market to be sold at a "reasonable price" so that speculators could not make excess profits by unduly depriving people of food. By the mid-17th century, these measures linked to "the moral economy of the commonweal in times of dearth" had ceased to operate, although calls for control of speculation carried on in the countryside throughout the 18th century as the "nature of things" was increasingly associated with the "Employment of Capital" for which emergency measures against starvation would only "aggravate the distress which it pretends to alleviate ...[27]

In positing this new rational path based on the "Employment of Capital," the evangelical proselytizers of economics ignored the mountain of evidence of inequality and suffering, traveling down-stream as they were on the raft of free enterprise. As E. P. Thompson states concerning the repeal of restrictions on the corn trade in the 18th century and the views which underwrote their repeal:

> This signified less a new model [of political economy] than an anti-model — a direct negative to the disintegrating Tudor policies of "provision". "Let every act that regards

the corn laws be repealed", wrote Arbuthnot in 1773; "Let corn flow like water, and it will find its level". The "unlimited, unrestrained freedom of the corn trade" was also the demand of Adam Smith. The new economy entailed a demoralizing of the theory of trade and consumption no less-far reaching than the more widely-debated dissolution of the restrictions upon usury.[28]

The common weal was now considered to be protected by the "de-moralized" *laissez-faire* workings of the market, rather than being protected by moral and religious restrictions. This is not to suggest that Smith was immoral or not concerned with public good, but as Thompson point out, that "the new political economy was disinfested of intrusive moral imperatives" and where "the natural operation of supply and demand in the free market would maximize the satisfaction of all parties and establish the common good."[29] In this preoccupation with the judicious workings of the market, those who supported the expansion of the market denigrated any protests to the rise and fall of food prices as being bereft of any moral perspective and instead were seen in reductionist terms as "rebellions of the belly."[30] This denigration of protest served the purpose of masking the fact that supply and demand were not necessarily serving the common good as much as they were serving the merchants who self-consciously manipulated the market in corn. In the next chapter, I will link this reductionist conception of resistance to market relations to the debate over "environmental security" and the increasing paranoia and denigration expressed by capitalist interests as related to the starving brigands from the South.

If the expansion of market relations had only to be accounted for in terms of the obstacles it had to overcome (assuming its existence in order to explain its coming into being, as Wood argues), it is my intention to contrast moral arguments linked to questions of community in the usury debate and the sustainability debate. The sense of "obstacle" associated with the clerics who resisted the movement towards an economy that had autonomy from God, law, and community in the usury debate signals the gradual removal of all impediments to the workings of market economy throughout modernity, to a point now, in the context of the emphasis on global economic competitiveness, where there is a denigration of any protest to the extension of the logic of the market. In response to concerns over environmental issues, a self-conscious moral component associated with the strongest definitions of sustainability have been set out which would attempt to restrict the free rein of economics, and relocate resource exploitation within a broader societal frame of "social values." Environmental concerns therefore offer the opportunity to engage in self-conscious obstructionism by claiming that there is a social frame of reference which can supersede the economic frame of reference.

SUSTAINABILITY AND THE AMORTIZATION OF HUMAN-NATURE RELATIONS

> [There is] the possibility that the insightful (and inciteful) potential of the concept of sustainability might be quickly reduced by co-option by the very kind of world view which brought us here in the first place. I am troubled by the possibility that sustainability might become the student rather than the teacher of economic concepts.
>
> John Ferguson[31]

This opportunity to contextualize the economic perspective in terms of "moral economy" exists in the current sustainability debate, in that there is a general acceptance that sustainability is a moral and ethical concept having to do with inter-generational and intra-generational equity. While there is general agreement that sustainability is a moral concept, the range of points of view that exist in the debate have to do with whether capitalist relations are the "student" or the "teacher" in this project. At one extreme are those economists such as Wilfred Beckerman who see the sustainability debate as all but identical with the "maximization of welfare" and therefore the addressing of environmental problems only requires "the old-fashioned economist's concept of optimality."[32] At the other extreme is the claim of Gustavo Esteva that "the creation of economic value requires the disvaluing of all other forms of social existence,"[33] which, in turn, requires an analytic and political challenge directed at powerful hegemonic forces. At one extreme is "consumer choice" of "green products," at the other is resistance by peasants to the privatization of common land.

An example of these contrasting points of view related to whether sustainability is about resolving environmental issues or solving historical forces can be presented by contrasting differing conceptions of the relationship between conservation and development as set out in discussions of the environmental movement leading up to the *World Conservation Strategy* (1980). Geographer Bruce Mitchell presents the history in this way:

> When the environmental movement was reaching its initial peak in the late 1960s a situation developed in which those concerned about protecting the natural environment became the opponents of those concerned with economic development and growth. This polarization of views led to many confrontations between the two groups ... as time went by, those supporting environmental quality issues created a credibility problem for themselves by consistently opposing development ... During the 1980s, a significant shift in thinking appeared. The idea was presented that sustained regional economic growth and ecological integrity were complimentary. This idea appeared at the core of the *World Conservation Strategy* ...[34]

Donald Worster refers to the same history in the relations between conservation and development, but from a very different perspective:

> Back in the 1960s and 1970s, when contemporary environmentalism first emerged, the goal was more obvious and the route more clear before they became obscured by political compromising. The goal was to save the living world around us, millions of species of plants and animals, including humans, from destruction by our own technology,

population, and appetites. The only way to do that, it was easy enough to see was to think the radical thought that there must be limits to growth in three areas — limits to population, limits to technology, and limits to appetite and greed. Underlying this insight was the growing awareness that the progressive, secular materialist philosophy on which modern life rests ... is deeply flawed and ultimately destructive to ourselves and the whole fabric of life on the planet ... Since it was so painfully difficult to make this turn, to go in a diametrically opposite direction from the way we had been going, however, many started looking for a less intimidating way. By the mid-1980s such an alternative, called 'sustainable development,' had emerged. First it appeared in the *World Conservation Strategy* ...[35]

These contrasting descriptions of the same period in the history of the environmental movement present conservation, on the one hand, as a regulatory problem solvable within capitalist relations, and on the other, as a social and cultural project which requires a profound redefinition of the relationship between humans and the rest of nature. The central issue here in the relationship between conservation and development rests on terms such as integration and complimentarity versus those of "diametrically opposed" challenge and resistance.

What is defining in these two histories — and I believe this is key to understanding all discussions of conservation — is how development is understood. If development is a "good thing" — as, for example, defined as "improving the quality of human life" in the *World Conservation Strategy* — then conservation need not be very exigent or challenging, and therefore can "compliment" development by dealing with specific difficulties which cause environmental problems. But if the hue of development darkens, if there are implicit assumptions about development which cause inequity and over-exploitation, then necessarily, the conceptions of conservation become more resistant, as they challenge many of the assumptions under which development operates. Therefore, conceptions of conservation are entirely dependent on what is understood as "economic development."

Both Mitchell and Worster present similar twists and turns to this short history of conservation, but it is very clear that Mitchell has a far less problematic conception of economic development than does Worster. Indeed, environmentalists "created a credibility problem for themselves by continually opposing development." Therefore, what the environmental movement required for credibility was the adoption of the paradigm of development in which "economic growth and ecological integrity" have a "complimentary" relationship, rather than one of "polarization."

By contrast, Worster sees this trajectory in terms of co-option and "political compromising" rather than complimentarity, where the path to ecological integrity seemed to difficult and "diametrically opposed" to "deeply flawed" and "ultimately destructive" forces present in modern industrial society. Whereas for Mitchell, the values underlying conservation and the values underlying development are all but identical, for Worster the life of "material simplicity and spiritual richness" are in sharp contrast to the "greed" associated with development. So as the assumptions of development become more problematic, and the contrasting assumptions of conservation become more challenging, the articulation of an alternate vision to the one of the dominant forces of development becomes a necessary aspect of the conservation project.

Those who do not question the assumptions of modern economy — for example, economists such as Beckerman who see environmentalists as redundant to a analysis better done by "old fashioned" economics — tend to denigrate the "credibility" of those who continue to resist the priorities of development. As opposed to this denigration of protest, which Thompson outlines in the repeated portrayal of mob responses in terms of "rebellions of the belly," there is an alternate perspective which can be linked to moral economy. The question that arises here is: Do conceptions of the moral aspects of sustainability provide such an alternate perspective which can offer some hope for environmental concerns through challenging development imperatives?

To begin to answer this question, it is useful to begin with the most commonly accepted definition that comes from the United Nations Commission leading to the creation of *Our Common Future*: sustainability is "development that meets the needs of the present without compromising the ability of future generations to meet their needs."[36] What is abundantly clear when this definition of sustainability comes up against Wood's analysis of capitalism, is that to link development with the meeting of "needs" is entirely insufficient in terms of understanding what is going on in the world today with regard to economic globalization, as discussed in the previous chapter. The insufficiency of this definition of sustainability is illustrated by Chatterjee and Finger's argument that as a result of the United Nations process leading up to the Rio Conference, the rich got richer and the poor got poorer, and the planet was degraded in the process. If what capitalism is about is the privatization of political power in the economic realm, and the pumping of surplus labour out of humans and pumping surplus resources out of nature, then a viable environmental initiative has to address these processes. So not only does the "needs" conception of sustainability fail in terms of negotiation and implementation of its agenda, it has also failed in analytical terms.

These contrasting conceptions of sustainability linked to integration and complimentarity, on the one hand, and resistance and challenge on the other, can also be conveyed in terms of internalizing externalities on the one hand, and externalizing internalities on the other. With regard to the project of internalizing externalities, Michael Jacobs states:

> Most of the academic work done in environmental economic may be described as an attempt to incorporate the environment into the conventional or "neoclassical" framework of economic analysis. The environment is perceived as a set of commodities ... valued like other commodities by individuals in society. But because environmental commodities are usually available free (that is at zero price), this value generally goes unrecognized. The result is that they get overused, leading to environmental degradation. To bring the environment into the economic calculus, prices or monetary values therefore need to be assigned to the various goods and services it provides.[37]

This environmental project regards the expansion of the valuations of capitalism as incomplete and therefore have to be expanded so that market failure can be overcome. For example, *Our Common Future* sets out three areas that have to be addressed by sustainability: between economics and environment, between poverty and the environment, and between political systems and the environment. As Ferguson argues, mainstream economics offers to solve these problems without undue challenge to the dominant structures of capitalism:

> first, by monetarily realizing the instrumental value of nature; second, by maximizing wealth and making sure that utility is maximized from finite amounts of resources; and third, by providing people with property rights to protect the ecological integrity of their surroundings.[38]

Internalizing externalities therefore makes use of instrumental valuation, wealth maximization and privatarianism in property rights to promote a sustainability agenda, all of which convert more and more of the world into categories that are commensurable to market relations, thereby extending the "totalizing logic of capitalism."

What this acceptance amounts to is the universalization of market values as the basis of both analysis of environmental problems, as well as the strategies to ameliorate them. The market is both the problem and the solution, or more precisely, what is required to overcome environmental problems is the extension of the market to include realities which have hitherto been external to it. In the Foreword to *Green Markets: The Economics of Sustainable Development* by Theodore Panayotou, Oscar Arias states that:

> There is a fundamental relationship between these disciplines [ecology and economics], given the exchanges that occur between complex communities of producers and consumers. Nothing is given away for free; everything is sold ... Natural capital was not treated as a conventional form of capital and thus its depreciation and maintenance requirements were not included in economic calculations ...

environmental costs must be internalized rather than transferred to future generations.[39]

This kind of claim is the cornerstone of environmental economics, repeated like a catechism. Panayotou goes on to state that "excessive environmental damage" is caused by "distorted markets that set inappropriate prices for natural resources. Sustainable development, therefore, requires that government correct these market failures and reform policies."[40] From this perspective, the central issue is the possible difficulties environmental problems might pose if the market is not allowed to operate as it should.

With regard to the importance of biological diversity, Panayotou states:

> Diversity of species and environments is essential to long-term productivity and sustainability of economic development. Its preservation is a form of investment for the future or insurance against future uncertainties.[41]

What is clear from these comments is that environmental concerns are important so that economic development can continue. Overcoming environmental problems requires the extension of the categories of modern economy, rather than the questioning of them. Environmental problems are caused by the insufficient monetization of environmental aspects of the economy. Once again, the problem with human-nature relations is that they are not capitalist *enough*.

By contrast, the project of externalizing internalities would challenge these abstractions of exploitation as the sources of social and ecological failure, and set out a project which would overcome the "disvaluing of other forms of social existence" which economic valuation imposes. Wolfgang Sachs conveys the ensnarement of debate within the paradigm of "competitive productivism" as a "civilizational impasse" which occurs when the assumptions of economic development are insufficiently problematized.[42] If the ethical aspects of sustainability are to be effective, there will have to be a moral economy perspective which supersedes that of market economy.

CONCLUSION

In the broad sweep of the comparison of the usury debate and the sustainability debate, there is a kind of reverse symmetry. Within the historical context of the usury debate, capitalism had begun in early Modern England among the less secure merchants and tenant farmers, that is, those who did not have secure position or title to agricultural land and therefore had an interest in increased production associated with the "culture of improvement." They were opposed by clerics and religious leaders in the name of deeply-rooted values linked to community, and many of these advocates held secure positions within traditional structures of authority. Within the historical context of the sustainability debate, opposition exists between powerful economic interests which dominate the world and grant primacy to market relations; and those much less powerful environmental and community groups in the North and South who argue that there is social and ethical connection between humans and between humans and nature which overrides economic interests. The tables have therefore been turned in the relationship between economy and society, where, in the usury debate, wider social institutions were perceived to be, at least for a time, more powerful than emergent economic interests, while, in the sustainability debate, there is no question that economic concerns entirely dominate social perspectives which would argue for alternate trajectories than the one set out by market logic.

I have attempted to highlight this alternate perspective in the discussion of the sins of usury as set out by the Christian Church at the beginning of modernity. This alternate perspective also appeared at various moments of rapid expansion in capitalism as counter-movements associated with, among many, Levelers, Luddism, trade unions, democracy, feminism, socialism, non-aligned states, and environmentalism. What defines the forms of protest listed here are not so much their complimentarity to industrial capitalism, as the incommensurability of their contrasting values and relationships.

Dominique Temple points to this incommensurability of the relations between conservation and development in dramatic terms in his discussion of the relations between the Kanak people of the South Pacific island of New Caledonia and the French Colonial Government. Temple describes the absorption of the local culture of the Kanak into the Western paradigm of economic exchange as the "Policy of the Severed Flower"[43] which amputates Kanak culture from its roots in the "reciprocity of the gift" as the basis of social relations. If I began this chapter with the incommensurability of the sin of usury and the beginnings of capitalism within the history of Northern economic development, the chapter ends with the incommensurability of a local Pacific culture and colonial domination. Temple asks the question: "Can the economy of reciprocity be reduced to an exchange economy?" and observes:

> That is obviously what Westerners try to do, for if the
> categories of the economy of reciprocity can be interpreted
> as categories of the exchange economy, then one system
> is reducible to the other and one can integrate the Kanak
> system into the economic system that Western society is
> trying to impose on the whole world ... But if the answer is
> in the negative ... all integration to a Western political
> economy. . . can be seen as suicide or treason ... The roots
> of Kanak values are replaced with those of Western val-
> ues.[44]

As opposed to Western exchange, which is linked to accumulation, the reciprocity of Kanak gift giving is "an occasion to participate in the social being, in the communitarian being begotten by this form of reciprocity."[45] In the culture of reciprocity, money is an expression of prestige which "represents being and alliance" and "obliges one to give, to redistribute" as opposed to taking and accumulating. I wonder what environmental economics would look like if it conceived of economic valuation as representing "being and alliance." It is necessary to link conceptions of moral economy with sustainability if there is to be any hope of addressing environmental concerns. As opposed to pumping surplus labour out of humans and surplus resources out of nature, a project that can be described as externalizing internalities offers a potential challenge to the increasing internalization of political power in the economy. If the capitalist project has been to expand the realm of economic logic, and to transfer a large share of a society's political power to the privatized relations of the economy, the sustainability project associated with internalizing externalities merely extends and aids in that expansionary project, and therefore cannot sufficiently challenge appropriation and domination in capitalist relations. A more resistant and challenging conception of sustainability associated with externalizing internalities attempts to reclaim the political power buried internally in the economy, and externalize it so that it can return to the political and social realm, thereby opening up the opportunity for the creation of a moral economy.

NOTES

1   Norman Jones. 1989. *God and the Moneylenders*. Cambridge: Basil Blackwell, pp. 26–27.
2   John Cassidy. 1996. "The Decline of Economics," *The New Yorker*, Dec. 2, pp. 50–51.
3   R. H. Tawney. 1980. *Religion and the Rise of Capitalism*. Harmondsworth: Penguin, pp. 272–73.
4   Michael Jacobs. 1993. *The Green Economy: Environment, Sustainable Development and the Politics of the Future*. Vancouver: University of British Columbia Press, p. 77.
5   Jacobs. (1993:79).
6   Jones. (1989:4).
7   James C. Scott. 1976. *The Moral Economy of the Peasant: Rebellion and Subsistence in Southeast Asia*. New Haven: Yale University Press.
8   Jones. (1989:1).
9   Jones. (1989:1).
10   Jones. (1989:4).
11   Jones. (1989:19).
12   Jones. (1989:28).
13   Jones. (1989:20).
14   Benjamin Nelson. 1969. *The Idea of Usury*. Chicago: University of Chicago Press.
15   Jones. (1989:30,34).
16   Henry Rowlands, 1610. In Jones. (1989:145).
17   Roger Hacket, 1591. In Jones. (1989:146).
18   Jones. (1989:147).
19   Jones. (1989:149).

20   Walter Howse, 1605. In Jones (1989:157).

21   Jones. (1989:174).

22   Christopher Hill. 1974. *The World Turned Upside Down*. Harmondsworth: Penguin.

23   R. H. Tawney. 1925. "Introduction" to *A Discourse Upon Usury* by Thomas Wilson. New York: Harcourt Brace, p. 17.

24   Tawney. (1925:22).

25   Tawney. (1925:24–25).

26   E. P. Thompson. 1971. "The Moral Economy of the English Crowd in the Eighteenth Century," *Past and Present*, No. 50, p. 108.

27   Thompson. (1971:131).

28   Thompson. (1971:89).

29   Thompson. (1971:90).

30   Thompson. (1971:77).

31   John Ferguson. 1996. *What Sustains Sustainability? An Examination of Economic Visions of Sustainability*. PhD Dissertation. Toronto: Graduate Programme in Social and Political Thought, York University, p. 18.

32   Wilfred Beckerman. 1994. "'Sustainable Development': Is it a Useful Concept?," *Environmental Values*. Vol. 3, p. 195

33   Gustavo Esteva. 1992. "Development." In *The Development Dictionary*. Wolfgang Sachs [Ed.]. London: Zed Books, p. 18.

34   Bruce Mitchell. 1989. *Geography and Resource Analysis*. New York: Longman and Wiley, p. 302.

35   Donald Worster. 1993. "The Shakey Ground of Sustainability." In *Global Ecology: A New Arena of Political Conflict*. Wolfgang Sachs [Ed.]. London: Zed Books, pp. 132–33.

36   Gro Harlem Brundtland. 1987. *Our Common Future*. New York: Oxford University Press, p. 43.

37   Jacobs. (1993:xv).

38   Ferguson. (1996:208).

39   Oscar Arias. 1993. "Foreword" to *Green Markets: The Economics of Sustainable Development* by Theodore Panayotou. San Francisco: Institute for Contemporary Studies Press, p. ix–x.

40   Panayotou. (1993:2).

41   Panayotou. (1993:4).

42   Wolfgang Sachs. 1992. "Environment." In *The Development Dictionary*. Wolfgang Sachs [Ed.]. London: Zed Books, p. 39.

43   Dominique Temple. 1988. "The Policy of the Severed Flower," *INTERculture*, Vol. 98, Winter, pp. 10–35.

44   Temple. (1988:14,16).

45   Temple. (1988:18).

IV

Are Environmentalists Hysterical or Paranoid?: Capitalism and "Environmental Security"

The apparent denigration in the title of this chapter is meant to draw attention to the relationship between representations of environmental issues and economic realities, especially in the context of disagreement, where contested realities are represented in dramatically different ways by various interests concerned with environmental issues. What is clear in the context of these disagreements is that "ownership" of the issue has significant ramifications for not only understanding the causes of problems, but also for what to do about them. What is becoming increasingly apparent is that — from the point of view of those groups who have not been fully absorbed into capitalist relations — the solutions presented by most sustainability initiatives amount to little more than strengthening the forces which cause appropriation and domination.

Benchmark for this analysis is the increasingly common appearance of the word "security" in the titles of articles and books dealing with environmental issues. Concerns are expressed with regard to "food security," "security of resources," and the more generic "environmental security," among many. Indeed, the United States Central Intelligence Agency now has an environmental department. What interests me, then, is the significance of the increasing appearance of the word "security" — as represented in the work of analysts such as Thomas Homer-Dixon — for human communities and natural communities, and the way the concern for security minimizes any analysis of capitalist relations, and at the same time, the term tends to render as invalid those cultures which cause security problems by resisting incursions of capital. It is my intention to link the denigration of protest that E. P. Thompson described in the last chapter in terms of "rebellions of the belly" with the way environmental security perspectives tend to confirm the increasing domination of capitalist relations, as set out in the "New Barbarism thesis." I contend that the work of analysts such as Thomas Homer-Dixon represent a closing down of possibility offered by the sustainability debate, and the entrenchment of competitive interests who are concerned about environmental issues in order to protect the very economic interests which caused the environmental problems in the first place.

INTERIORITY AND ENVIRONMENTALISM

The overarching argument of this book originates in the problematization of the historical relations in capitalism where there is a separation of the political and the economic spheres which, in turn, leads to dynamics of appropriation and domination where surplus labour is pumped out of humans and surplus resources out of nature. There is, then, a historical specificity to the fracture of interiority and exteriority in human experience and the fracture between human history and natural history in more collective terms which have to be understood as being aspects of appropriation and domination in capitalism. It is not that a sense of interiority of experience or a fracture between humans and the rest of nature had not existed previous to capitalism. The transformation from the Paleolithic society of hunter-gatherers to the Neolithic domestication of plants and animals was just as important in this regard. But in the context of addressing environmental problems, it is the forces of capitalism which have to be challenged currently.

Representing humans and nature in terms of labour and resources — which is a common occurrence in global management discourse — locates the environmental crisis within a broader crisis of modernity in which viable conceptions of human identity and nature are undermined by the structures and processes of late capitalism, and result in the contemporaneousness of the "death of the human subject" and "end of nature" discussions.[1] I will argue that environmental security concerns operate within these increasingly impoverished conceptions of human identity and nature.

At the same time as there have been an increasing prevalence of security concerns with regard to the environment, there have also been a spate of books by moderate environmentalists engaged in "green-bashing" the more radical discussions of environmental issues.[2] I believe both these trends reflect the intensification of the forces of economic globalization which are rendering the world into categories which suit those expanding realities and undermines significant analysis of the relationship between those realities and current environmental problems.

In order to get at these contrasting and conflictive views of environmental issues, I will examine current works on environmentalism in terms of psychological conditions characterized in terms of hysteria and paranoia. I will discuss hysteria as a negative category used in condemning the "failures of the uninitiated." Broadly speaking, hysteria can be defined as the pathology linked to the over identification with those around you in the context of a differential in power relationships "in which the ego is constantly being overwhelmed by the products of the illness."[3] Questions therefore arise concerning what has happened to the world so that identifying with those around you in collective terms is rendered into a social pathology.

Specifically, I am going to highlight Aihwa's Ong's argument in *Spirits of Resistance and Capitalist Discipline*[4] in which Malay factory women have hysterical fits on the factory shop-floor as a form of passive resistance to transformations in identity related to the immersion in the work discipline of capitalism. I will link the concern for "environmental security" with the fact that peasant women who experience three hysterical fits were fired from the factory for "security reasons."[5]

I am aware that the term hysteria has a long and complex history,[6] but for my specific purposes here, I am using the phenomenon of hysteria as it appears in response to the expansion of capitalist relations, and as it records what Roy Porter describes as "a history [of hysteria] in which the very notions of mind and body, and the boundaries between them, are constantly being challenged and reconstituted."[7] I believe that hysteria not only records changes in mind-body boundaries, but also the boundaries between self and other, of being in the world.

By contrast, security concerns that are successfully "initiated" into the dominant categories of late capitalism, will be associated with particular readings of paranoia. Specifically, I am going to examine Ernest Becker's essay "Paranoia: The Poetics of the Human Condition"[8] in terms of what he describes as the negative interest a powerful world takes in individuals who feel weak and helpless. I will associate this kind of representation of human identity with being driven indoors in late capitalism, an impulse which is emblematic of the devitalized condition associated with surveillance and control.

David Orr sets out a similar contrast in perspectives to hysteria and paranoia when he describes conservation perspectives in terms of biophilia and development perspectives in terms of biophobia.[9] For Orr, biophobia is a social pathology similar to paranoia, and which is directly related to modern development, forming the "foundation for the politics of exploitation." Biophobia is underwritten by a contempt for nature and animated connection to other beings, and expresses itself in terms such as "bottom line," "progress," "costs and benefits," and "economic growth."[10] By contrast, biophilia is defined as "the urge to affiliate with other forms of life." In other words, biophilia is the urge to identify with those around you, a condition of mental and physical health, which Orr argues is not innate but depends on relational context. Whereas in the past, those tribes which were biophobic or incompetent in relational terms "passed into oblivion through starvation or disease," this is no longer the case because technology has enabled modern society to engineer survival and put off, at least temporarily, the ecological and social consequences of this historical trajectory.

In the conclusion to the book, I am going to explore the possibility of creating a socially-viable conception of human-nature relations in which, to quote naturalist John Livingston, "all participants are subjects."[11] This returns the moral economy discussion to a necessarily more egalitarian and symmetrical basis in which no one group dominates, and no "others" are exploited or objectified. In turn, this metaphor of care can present a profound challenge to the structures and processes of late capitalism in which concern is increasingly expressed in terms of securing resources for powerful interests in the name of profit, that is, in securing the participation of objects, which, in turn, reinforces domination, exploitation, and objectification.

My intention in using terms such as hysteria and paranoia, or biophilia and biophobia, is to highlight that what we call consciousness is what the world has laid claim to. In this sense, I believe there is a connection between the unconscious and wilderness. Both are "animated elsewheres" which account for, and sometimes allow for, the misery here. Within this fracture, there is a tendency to almost fetishize the multi-valenced qualities of those dislocated projections — as with the unconscious in psychoanalysis or in the "deep ecology" of wilderness preservation — which can confirm the split between the repression and superficiality of "the everyday," as well as deflect analysis away from a consideration of relations in the heart of culture which would overcome this fracture.

HYSTERIA: THE FAILURES OF THE UNINITIATED

> This inquiry deals with struggles over the means and meanings of gender in the context of exchange, disjunctions, and conflicts generated by land dispossession and the subjugation of peasants to new forms of control and domination.
>
> Aihwa Ong[12]

In his book *Madness and Modernism*, Louis Sass describes schizophrenia as a condition which is directly related to the "struggles" of modern realities in which "dispossessions" in the external world are connected to the de-animation of experience in which we are thrown back on ourselves:

> The delusions of schizophrenics are not failures of reasoning, but of appropriate feeling ... Madness ... is 'to be sure, a self-deceiving condition, but one that is generated from within rationality rather than by a loss of rationality' ... Attention is focused on the field of consciousness itself and we seem to experience experience.[13]

Ong defines discipline as "the effect [on the individual] of the exercise of power ... and the enforced and induced compliance with the political, social, and economic objectives, considered rational and functional for capitalist production."[14] In this regard, I believe it is possible to associate what Sass describes as madness being "generated from within rationality" and the connection that rationality might have with the work discipline in capitalism. Ong chronicles the experience of Malay factory women as they move from *kampung* peasant culture to the newly-constructed industrial factories. This movement from one set of relations to another is punctuated by *hantu* spirit possessions which result is epidemics of fits and "fugue states" among the women on the shop-floor, and evokes lives caught between non-capitalist morality and capitalist discipline. The highlighting of crisis and dislocation at the moment of entry into capitalist relations allows for a more significant problematization of late modern realities, recognizing that the incursion of economic relations into personal experience results in a "loss of appropriate feeling" in the context of "control and domination." It is this crisis in human identity which can illustrate what Wood has described as the invisible coercion of the economy.

By contrast, those who operate the factories characterize these fits in terms of hysteria, thereby pathologizing and individualizing these conditions, and denying them their social significance. It is this denigration of the "failures of the uninitiated" which is important for discussions of environmental problems. Within the contested reality of historical transformations in modes of production, these hysterical fits provide an evocative representation of the link between analysis and interests which can be applied to the debate over environmental issues. In these terms, I believe there is a link between the historical realities which support the expanding discipline of capitalism and those who characterize the environmental debate in terms of security. The separation of the political-social sphere from the economic sphere which occurs in the context of accelerated capitalist expansion results in this loss of experiential viability in external social relations due to the work discipline of capitalism.

Sass states that hysterical psychosis "have occurred at times in epidemic proportions among ethnic groups facing massive social change,"[15] and he describes these states in this way:

Hysterical reactions such as amnesia, fugue states, brief fits of frenzy, and paroxysmal behavioural outbursts seem to have become rare in the industrialized world, yet they remain hallmarks of mental disorder in Africa and perhaps elsewhere in the Third World, occurring far more frequently than do the internalizing states that have a comparable importance in the West.[16]

Of importance here is the recognition that hysteria is linked to historical change. In Freud's early work, there is a predominance of case studies of hysteria in female patients. These conditions have now all but disappeared in Western women as they have been initiated into the character armour which Sass relates to "internalizing states" in the West. This disappearance has been challenged by critics such as Elaine Showalter who argue that the media — given its hybrid position between internal and external experience — have continued to generate symptoms of mass hysteria with regard to "fad" illnesses.[17]

Within medical literature, there has, however, been a consistent decline in reported cases of hysteria throughout the twentieth century. In his historical study *Approaching Hysteria: Disease and its Interpretations*, Mark Micale states that:

> … hysteria in our own time — both the medical diagnosis and the pathological entity the diagnosis designates — is believed greatly to have dwindled in frequency. Clinicians working in many different countries and institutional settings and within diverse theoretical systems have reported a sharp and continuing decline in the incidence of the disorder throughout the twentieth century.[18]

Micale goes on to state that: "Interestingly, the progressive semantic suppression of hysteria by official psychiatric organizations in the past half century"[19] has led to the emergence of what he refers to a "the new hysteria studies" in fields such as feminism where the pathologizing of female experience has significant ramifications for modern gender relations. Like other categories of subjective experience, hysteria has disappeared into the fractured specializations of "factitious illness disorder," "dissociative disorder — conversion type," and "psychogenic pain disorder." The reclamation of this lost history can aid in the reclamation of alternate forms of social relations in which the internalized character armour of modernity is seen to arise in the context of increasingly rigid and disciplined relations in capitalism. Indeed, the internalized character armour is the part of experience that has been laid claim to by capitalism.

"THE GHOSTS DISTURB ONLY THE NEW GIRLS"

> Cultural change is not understood as unfolding according to some predetermined logic (of development, modernization, or capitalism) but as the disrupted, contradictory, and differential outcomes which involve changes in identity, relations of struggle and dependence, including the experience of reality itself.
>
> Aihwa Ong[20]

Ong relates these hysterical episodes experienced by factory workers to changes in the lives of peasant Malay women as they enter the factory routine:

> Induction to capitalist relations of production generates profound contradictions in the Malay peasants' orientation toward work and life. Hitherto, village life was ordered by the rhythm of agricultural cycles, daily Islamic prayers, and *kampung* tasks largely carried out according to personal compulsion; everyday life was decidedly noncapitalist ... Thus, I would argue, the trauma of industrial labor for village women is the rigidity of the work routine, continual male supervision, and a devaluation of their labor in the factory. Spirit possession episodes, in which the women become violent and scream abuses, are to be deciphered ... as a protest against the loss of autonomy/humanity in work.[21]

The rural Malay universe is "inhabited by spirits which move easily between human and nonhuman domains," and these spirits become, for Ong, part of the "unconscious retaliation against male authority ... [and] a sense of dislocation in human relations" which she relates to a "twentieth-century homelessness."[22]

What Ong's analysis does is move discussions of hysteria from individual pathology to a recognition of its historical locatedness within differentials in power relations. What becomes clear is that, when focusing on the anxiety and grief of these hysterical fits, these historical transformation to industrialism reflect a disruption in a set of relations that were already in place in *kampung* culture:

> In trans-national corporations, we see that relations of domination and subordination, constituted in scientific terms, operate not only through the overt control of workers' bodies but in the way young females comes to see themselves. In their changing positions within the family, the village, the labor process, and wider society, they devise counter tactics for resisting images imposed on them and come to construct their own images.[23]

What is important here is that it is individual human conceptions of "experience" which forms the basis of repression and control when "local meanings, values, and practices have been reworked within the operations of administrative organs, capitalist enterprises, and civil institutions."[24] The lack of consent expressed in the fits comes from the incompleteness of the disciplining project. It comes from those who are not properly initiated, and who therefore require special attention from medical experts.

This new world of surveillance and discipline is in sharp contrast to *kampung* peasant life:

> The overzealous villager seen cycling to his garden on a hot afternoon is mocked as "devil-driven" by neighbors jealous that he is planting capital while they take their customary nap.[25]

It is this trauma of transformation which Ong characterizes as a "local drama which momentarily suggests universal features of cultural change in the late twentieth century."[26]

This same trauma is conveyed during specific periods in the evolution of capitalism in Europe. In 19th century France, at the Salpetriere women's hospital, two-thirds of the hysterical patients were working-class women when, by 1866, they made up one-third of the labour force. As Martha Noel Evans comments:

> Poor women were thrust into a new and often disorienting freedom in urban centres. Alone, unsupported by the family groups they were accustomed to, often paid below subsistence wages, they faced a stressful lot.[27]

Indeed other peasant and pastoral people have a similar sense of daily tasks which contrast those of capitalism. As E. E. Evans-Pritchard states with regard to the Nuer people of Africa:

> The daily timepiece is the cattle clock, the round of pastoral tasks, and the time of day and the passage of time through the day are to a Nuer primarily the succession of these tasks and their relations to one another.[28]

Or similarly in Algeria, Pierre Bourdieu describes the approach to the tasks of the day as one of "nonchalant indifference" in which "haste is seen as a lack of decorum combined with diabolical ambition."[29] E. P. Thompson describes similar transformations in work discipline leading up to the Industrial Revolution:

> Thus enclosure and agricultural improvement were both, in some sense, concerned with the efficient husbandry of the time of the labour-force ... [and] submission to a more exacting labour discipline ... [arising from] a greater sense of time-thrift among improving capitalist employers.[30]

In a broader Western context, Karl Polanyi conveys the "universal features" of the disruption of social relations in the movement toward industrialism in this way:

> We submit that an avalanche of social dislocation, surpassing by far the enclosure period, came down upon England; that this catastrophe was the accompaniment of a vast movement of economic improvement; that an entirely new institutional mechanism [the market] was starting to act on Western society ...[31]

Polanyi then goes on to state that:

> Machine production in a commercial society involves ... a transformation ... of the natural and human substance of society into commodities. The conclusion, though weird, is inevitable ... the dislocation caused by such devices must disjoint human relationships and threaten natural habitat with annihilation.[32]

The experience of the Malay factory women may be a concentrated and accelerated version of events which, in their aggregate, took place over several centuries in the West. These transformations in relations in the West were also punctuated by similar episodes of hysteria and resistant indolence as a register of disruption, which were similarly pathologized and denigrated by the proselytizers of efficiency and utility, as in this comparison of English and Irish workers:

> By the 1830s and 1840s it was commonly observed that the English industrial worker was marked off from his fellow Irish worker, not by a greater capacity for hard work, but by his regularity, his methodical paying-out of energy, and perhaps also by a repression, not of enjoyments, but of the capacity to relax in old, uninhibited ways.[33]

It is this transformation from "old, uninhibited ways" to the "paying-out of energy" which conveys the incursion of disciplining which alters conceptions of reality, and for our purposes more specifically, alters conceptions of environmental problems and what to do about them.

PARANOIA: CREATIVE INGENUITY FROM A DESPERATE POSITION

Paralleling Sass's contention that insanity is not the loss of reason, but rather, the end point of reason and "the loss of appropriate feeling," Ernest Becker begins his essay on paranoia by quoting G. K. Chesterton's statement that the "madman is not the man who has lost his reason. The madman is the man who has lost everything except his reason."[34] It is my intention to link the disappearance of "appropriate feeling" expressed in paranoid episodes with the expanding work discipline of capitalism.

Ernest Becker describes paranoia as "creative ingenuity from a desperate position" in which the impetus is to "put concern back in a world in which there is so little concern." The social-historical context for this desperate position is the modern representation of a weak and seemingly helpless individual who feels overwhelmed by a powerful and foreboding world. The "concern" in this world therefore is the necessarily negative interest that a powerful entity takes in doing harm to others.

Because of the loss of appropriate feeling in a world gone indoors, a world of "mind alone," there is the consequent ordering of the world described in terms of paranoid fantasies which "give the world form," even if that form is a threatening one. The personal threat is more reassuring than the depersonalizing realities of the modern world. As such, it is an impoverished attempt to reassert the personal into the depersonalized reality associated with surveillance and control.

Set out in these terms, Becker's central insight is that individual experience in industrial society appears untenable in terms of the relationship between an increasingly beleaguered self operating in an increasingly threatening world. But this is the last thing the self will admit, because it would break through the armoured mask of self-assurance that surrounds life-striving in an antagonistic world. To drop the pretense of self-sufficiency is to destroy the laboriously built up protection of the social self.

As opposed to archaic societies which inhabited a universe that was alive, moral, and personal and in which gods and spiritual beings of all kinds caused things to happen, and no event was casual or abstracted, the modern world is profoundly impersonal. In this context, paranoia represents the fact that people might prefer real enemies to the impersonality of threat in modern society. Bad things must happen because somebody cares and is out for control.

For Becker, the problem of identity is the problem of strength. It is precisely the aloneness of humans which Becker accepts as given and universal. This aloneness, I believe, needs to be historicized more clearly within modern social and economic relations, and the contrast those relations have with, for example, with *kampung* culture in Malaysia where "appropriate feeling" survives within community relations. To some extent, Becker points to this contrast in relations when he states that:

> ... if you are at ease and feel you belong your thoughts
> are generous, warm, broad, rich, tentative, and open. If you
> feel trapped and overwhelmed, your thoughts are mean,
> chilly, poor, humorless, dogmatic, and closed.[35]

He then goes on to state that the problem of mental health is a problem of organisms who are cramped, crippled, or blocked in their experience. A sane society loves the laughter of children, values pulsating life over mechanical things, whole organisms over part truths, new birth over old interests. Becker argues that no amount of frenzied thought or logic can give us these qualities, but that what is required is a "totally lived life." The concern here for my purposes is directed to the identification of the historical obstacles which stand in the way of that goal.

The Cold War was a prime example of paranoia, and the difficulty that the Cold War mentality had in putting itself at risk in order to transform itself into a more accommodating mentality. Even in the context of the crumbling of the U.S.S.R., it was very difficult for the other countries involved to begin to ratchet down the arms race. To give up on the negative interest of the arms race required other countries to do the most difficult thing, to trust, to yield, and be generous. The seeming intractability of current environmental problems can be understood in these terms: given the force of current historical realities, it may be that we will have to do the hardest thing in order to solve environmental problems.

ENVIRONMENTAL SECURITY AND THE DENIGRATION OF REBELLION

> ... the historical record is not a simple one of neutral and inevitable technological change, but is also one of exploitation and of resistance to exploitation; and that values stand to be lost as well as gained.
>
> E. P. Thompson[36]

In my discussion of hysteria and paranoia, I have tried to create a context for understanding the relationship between environmental security and subjective experience. In summary, I have presented hysteria as the recording of disturbance caused by the shift from rural peasant culture to industrial culture, while paranoia represents a response to the impoverished context of relations within modern industrial society. Central to this contrast between hysteria and paranoia is the differential in power relations which is resisted in hysteria, and accepted in paranoia. The hysterical fits are caused by the violation of symmetrical relations in rural culture, whereas paranoia confirms the helpless impoverishment of domination. Any attempt to challenge the increasing privatization of political power in the economy has to pass through and challenge, as it were, the impoverishment of human experience which goes along with that process: creative ingenuity from a desperate position.

Security concerns confirm and entrench the modern industrial relations within the environmental debate, and in doing so, short circuit the wider social and cultural debate which would historicize the current context of conservation discussions. Security perspectives presume a drive for control and dominance, they assume competition with others who have the same goal. They assume that there is a pervasive negative concern in the world, and that competition and force are necessary, given that resources are scarce and environmental security is a zero-sum game. In this sense, the appearance of security concerns confirms that the wider social and cultural debate which could accompany the environmental debate will not appear.

In his article "Environmental Scarcities and Violent Conflict," Thomas Homer-Dixon assesses the implications of "environmentally induced conflict for international security."[37] In terms of the negative interest that the world takes with regard to environmental concerns, Homer-Dixon begins the article by stating:

> Within the next fifty years ... scarcities of renewable resources will increase sharply. The total area of high-quality agricultural land will drop, as will the extent of forests and the number of species they sustain. Coming generations will also see the widespread depletion and degradation of aquifers, rivers, and other water resources; the decline of many fisheries; and perhaps significant climate change.[38]

He then asks the question: If such "environmental scarcities" become severe, could they precipitate "violent civil or international conflict?" Homer-Dixon answers in the affirmative by stating that:

> In brief, our research showed that environmental scarcities are already contributing to violent conflicts in many parts of the developing world. These conflicts are probably the early signs of an upsurge of violence in the coming decades that will be induced or aggravated by scarcity. The violence will usually be sub-national, persistent, and diffuse.[39]

The focus of his analysis is on the "developing world" as the source of conflict. This perspective shifts attention away from the "war" that is the standard practice of capitalism, and instead displaces analysis to the margins where the visible fallout occurs from this war. This "war" has been described by such theorists as Rees as "the appropriation of the carrying capacity" of post-colonial countries by the industrialized North. Homer-Dixon's depiction of "the upsurge of violence" which is "aggravated by scarcity" presents a similar crude reductionism which Thompson described in terms of "rebellions of the belly" caused by periodic shortages of corn in England. This attribution of the causes of conflict to competition for scarce resources and to "empty bellies" renders invisible, as Thompson points out, any consideration that there might be a moral and ethical basis to resistance, rather than just hunger and barbarism, which, in turn, might allow for a recognition that there is a viable politics of resistance to capitalism.

Instead, Homer-Dixon focuses on three dynamics which cause conflict, all of them generally associated with Southern countries: (1) conflict caused by competition over increasingly scarce resources (resource wars) due to environmental degradation; (2) "group identity" conflicts caused by movements of large segments of population resulting from environmental stress; and (3) environmental scarcity increases economic scarcity, disrupting social institutions and leading to civil strife.[40] Although Homer-Dixon sets out his concept of "environmental scarcity" to include considerations of populations growth and unequal distribution of resources, as well as the economic and technological forces which cause resource degradation, his example of unequal distribution of land and resources is the expropriation of the Miskito Indians by the Sandanista Government of Nicaragua in the name of a Marxist ideology where the Miskitos were viewed "as a backward people with a competing worldview and a precapitalist mode of production."[41]

Given that the general triumph of market-based economic globalization is the major exploitation initiative currently going on in the world — and the consequent environmental degradation and unequal distribution of resources which have accompanied this triumph — the use of this example seems to be a bit of a reach, and reflects an unease, I believe, on the part of Homer-Dixon to identify current dominant global market forces which cause "environmental scarcity." Indeed, if it is Marxist ideology which is causing marginalization of indigenous people currently, there is cause for great celebration, since obviously there is no longer any reason to worry about these issues in the aftermath of the Cold War.

By contrast, I would argue that it is the internalization of politics in the market economy of capitalism which creates a set of forces which, in their standard practice, represent a war on local culture and natural habitat. Challenging these forces is the project of environmentalism. The kind of analysis set out by Homer-Dixon tends to mask, rather than highlight, this recognition of the cause of environmental problems. Thompson conveys a similar failure of analysis in discussions of the "spasmodic" role of common people in "food riots":

> ... the common people can scarcely be taken as historical agents ... intrud[ing only] occasionally and spasmodically upon the historical canvas, in periods of sudden social disturbance. These intrusions are compulsive, rather than self-conscious or self-activating: they are simple responses to economic stimuli. It is sufficient to mention a bad harvest or a down-turn in trade, and all requirements of historical explanation are satisfied.[42]

Homer-Dixon follows the example of marginalization in Nicaragua with instances of environmental conflict in Senegal, Mauritania, the Arab West Bank, the Philippines, and Malaysia; leaving no doubt that the trouble spots are in "developing" countries. Although Homer-Dixon describes what he calls "resource capture" by "powerful elites," he does so in the context of Southern countries such as Senegal, and therefore any consideration that there might be a systematic appropriation of the carrying capacity of the South by the "powerful elites" of the North is not identified as one of the dominant forces of current exploitation patterns.

In response to the appearance of environmental problems and the accompanying social dislocation, Homer-Dixon advocates such measures as "rapidly exploiting the country's environmental resources and re-investing the profits in capital, industrial equipment, and skills to permit a shift to other forms of wealth creation" or "economic incentives like increases in resource prices," without explaining how that price increase would be achieved within the current pricing arrangements of groups such as the GATT. Homer-Dixon concludes his discussion of these measures by stating:

> If either strategy is to succeed, a society must be able to supply enough ingenuity at the right places and times. Two kinds are key. Technical ingenuity is needed to develop, for example, new agricultural and forestry technologies that compensate for environmental loss. Social ingenuity is needed to create institutions and organizations that buffer people from the effects of scarcity and provide the right incentives for technological entrepreneurs. Social ingenuity is therefore often a precursor to technical ingenuity.[43]

Rather than environmental problems requiring an analysis of the causes of over-exploitation, in the future, "... conservation tasks will be more urgent, complex, and unpredictable, driving up the need for technical ingenuity" and "solving these problems through market and other institutional innovations will require great social ingenuity."[44]

In Homer-Dixon's analysis, the "social and technical solutions to scarcity" revolve around the development of "productive resource centres, efficient markets, and capable states," with which, unfortunately, poorer countries are currently "underendowed." There is a direct connection between a reductionist approach to strife and a confirmation of the workings of capitalism as the only basis for a consideration of environmental problems. As opposed to the analysis I have set out, Homer-Dixon's argues that the cause of environmental problems exists on the margins and that the solution to environmental problems lies in the confirmation and extension of capitalist relations of market adaptation and technological ingenuity. Serge Latouche refers to the kind of analysis engaged in by Homer-Dixon as a "historical sleight of hand" where the North,

> ... which has destabilized the rest of the world by its imperialistic expansion, becomes destabilized in its turn. The North, having invaded the South, is under threat of inva-

sion by the sheer fact of numbers. Its wealth, acquired by
virtue of global integration, is threatened in turn by this
same integration.[45]

The "care" that is taken here is one which enhances the interests of industrial groups and pathologizes marginal groups who are engaging only in
spasmodic upheaval linked to scarcity, and who are not "self conscious
and self-activating" actors with their own ethical perspective and historical trajectory.

    In his conceptualization of environmental problems in these im-
poverished terms, Homer-Dixon is "doing the dirty work of globalization"
by confirming a form of analysis which renders invisible the global economic forces which pump surplus labour out of humans and surplus resources out of nature. Instead, what we get is the paranoid vision in
which, in the best case "command and control" security scenario, some
will walk the cliff-edge of ecological collapse for the rest of history, while
other, less fortunate, groups will fall to their ruin because they are
underendowed with capitalist institutions.

MARGINAL PERSPECTIVES ON THE COMING ANARCHY

Whereas Homer-Dixon concludes his discussion by confirming that conflict will tend to be "persistent, diffuse and sub-national" in Southern
countries, Paul Richards begins his analysis of conflict in Sierra Leone
with the heading "Small Wars in a post-Cold War world." It is here that the
similarity in the analysis of Richards and Homer-Dixon ends. Richard's
work — entitled *Fighting For The Rainforest: War, Youth, and Resources
in Sierra Leone* — sets out to challenge the environmental determinism of
critics such as Homer-Dixon, which he describes as operating from the
following assumptions:

> Here is violence driven by environmental and cultural im-
> peratives which the West has no hand in shaping, and
> now has no responsibility to try and contain [aside from
> protecting their own interests]. These violent urges are

politically meaningless and beyond the scope of conventional diplomacy or conciliation. They are best understood
as natural forces — the cultural consequences of a biological tendency by Africans to populate their countries to
the point of environmental collapse.[46]

Echoing Thompson's "rebellions of the belly" critique, Richards claims
this reductionist approach to the basis of protest at the margins has to do
with the "fear of the revenge of the enslaved and the dispossessed ..."
who therefore require continual denigration in order to confirm the position of those who might otherwise feel threatened by these actions.
Richards describes this compulsive analysis and commentary as the New
Barbarism thesis which is based on three ideas:

First, cultural identity is essential and durable ... and [d]if-
ferent cultures and civilizations are thereby prone to clash.
    Second, ... States have lost the monopoly of mili-
tary violence once underwritten by nuclear balance of ter-
ror ... [and] organizations [are] prepared to pursue armed
conflict independently of sovereign states and without
reference to international opinion.
    Third, culture clash, resource competition and en-
vironmental breakdown provoke a rash of small, localized
and essentially uncontrollable armed conflicts. Many are
anarchic disputes — i.e. apolitical events indistinguish-
able from banditry and crime. Insulation rather than intervention is the rational response of the major powers.[47]

There is a very close similarity to Richard's New Barbarism thesis and
Homer-Dixon's analysis of the sources of environmental security issues
outlined earlier: resource scarcity causes resource wars, movements of
population due to environmental degradation causes ethnic conflict, and
environmental scarcity causes the breakdown of social institutions, leading to civil strife and insurgency. The main focus of Richard's analysis is
on *The Atlantic Monthly* essay written by Robert Kaplan, and entitled

"The Coming Anarchy,"[48] in which Kaplan discusses the work of Homer-Dixon in positive terms, although Richards never comments on it directly.

Richards refutes Kaplan's claim that the war in Sierra Leone was caused by population pressure and environmental degradation. Contrary to the New Barbarism thesis, Richards claims that:

> In fact the war has a clear political context, and the belligerents have perfectly rational political aims, however difficult it may be to justify the levels of violence they employ in pursuit of these aims. The rebel leadership has a clear political vision of a reformed and accountable state.[49]

Richards argues that the war in Sierra Leone was caused by a "protracted, post-colonial, crisis of patrimonialism" and that

> New Barbarism should be resisted since it undermines respect for those hybrid aspects of the West African cultural heritage that might be of greatest potential value in making peace.[50]

The route out of the difficulties proposed by Richards is in sharp contrast to the "social and technical ingenuity" approach to solutions set out by Homer-Dixon. Once again, the universalization of capitalist relations leads to the denigration of any other social and cultural trajectory, except the one that passes through market economy. As opposed to this kind of analysis, Richards proposes "*in situ* analysis of why the war has happened and what local groups might do ... to arrive at sensible and durable solutions to the challenges of conciliation."[51] In this, local people are surely not "underendowed."

INTERNATIONAL POLITICAL ECONOMY AND THE ENVIRONMENT

> ... organized and institutionalized chaos stems from the increasingly liberalized economic structures of contempo-

rary capitalism ... Indeed, there is a revolution of the powerful against the weak.

Stephen Gill[52]

In contrast to the perspectives of critics such as Homer-Dixon and
Kaplan, who see chaos emerging in the margins, I would argue that the
chaos is being generated in the centre. Björn Hettne discusses this increasing uncertainty in terms of the relations between global economic
structures and the nation-state:

> The post-Westphalian logic of the state refers to the con-
> cept of an interstate system derived from the principles
> that scholars have attributes to the peace of Westphalia
> that concluded the Thirty years war in 1648: the sovereign
> independence of the state; each state being motivated in
> its international behaviour by a consistent national inter-
> est; the interstate system regulated by a balance of power
> among principle powers. There is necessarily a particular
> political rationality underlying this behaviour. The
> Westphalian rationality takes a particular state as the given
> guarantee for security as well as welfare. What is outside
> the state borders is chaos and anarchy. The disorder and
> turbulence people experience today comes with the real-
> ization that this guarantee can no longer be taken for
> granted. The post-Westphalian logic implies that the na-
> tion-state has lost much of its usefulness and that solu-
> tions to the problems of security and welfare must, therefore,
> be found in trans-national structures, global or regional.[53]

This approach to increasing uncertainty presents a very different picture
of coming anarchy than that set out by Homer-Dixon. As Hettne states
with regard to the causes of this global insecurity:

> Limited wars may still serve the purpose of asserting or
> denying hegemonic claims ... [h]owever, the emerging battle-

ground is economic competition, possibly between emerging trading blocs.[54]

What is clear here is that there is significant instability in the political context in global terms and this instability will have detrimental
effects on the environment, especially when the cause of that instability is
global economic competition engaged in by powerful corporate interests.
Rather than having environmental scarcity concerns focused on "local
wars" as a source of impending security threats, what is required instead
for viable environmental initiatives is a more complex understanding of
the politics of this "new world order." Robert Cox describes this politics as
a "hyper-liberal capitalism" which is

> characterized by a liberating of the private sector from state
> intervention. This particular relationship of state to soci-
> ety has been propagated by the institutions of the world
> economy (the IMF and World Bank) in the countries of
> Africa and Latin America caught in a debt trap. It was em-
> braced by countries of the former Soviet bloc as the fast
> track to capitalism.[55]

The current state of chaos and uncertainty has to do with capital's abhor-
rence for any community but itself. This destructiveness does not come
from a gang of teenagers with machine guns, but from the standard practice of modern economy:

> The key criterion today is competitiveness; and derived
> from that are universal imperatives of deregulation,
> privatization, and the restriction of public intervention in
> economic processes. Neo-liberalism is transforming states
> from being buffers between external economic forces and
> the domestic economy into agencies for adapting domes-
> tic economies to the exigencies of the global economy. The
> results on a global level are ... greater polarization of rich

and poor, disintegration of pre-existing social bonds, and
alienation.[56]

As the role of nation-states are undermined, economic interests have increasingly globalized the production of goods and services. As well, these
processes are no longer circumscribed within the bureaucracies of big
trans-national corporations, but are increasingly managed by more flexible networks of productive entities which get organized around specific
projects. A consequence of this transformation in production is that the
core/periphery metaphor, which had a geographical connotation describing the dominant-subordinate relationship of national economies, now
applies more accurately to individual social relationships. There are many
fewer permanent employees in these corporations, and many more peripheral employees employed in "cottage industry" shops whose relationship
to the production process is more precarious. In the context of the increasing mobility of capital, large groups of people are therefore not effectively integrated within the global economy. As Cox argues, this results in
"the perception that much of the world's population is not needed by the
global economy" which, in turn, leads to "mass migration from South to
North and from East to West" and "environmental destruction."[57]

　　Here is a very different explanation for the causes of movement of
population, of civil strife, and environmental degradation in the South, as
compared with the New Barbarism thesis. This analysis lays the cause of
these problems squarely on the "self-expansion of capital." Rather than
the paranoid "fear of the revenge of the enslaved and dispossessed"
expressed by powerful interests, Cox argues for an *in situ* approach to
overcoming these difficulties:

> The reconstitution of society and political authority from
> the bottom up would require a different sense of the polity:
> one that put emphasis on arousing capacities for collec-
> tive action inspired by common purposes.[58]

In the terms set out here, the moral economy of the periphery can provide
the basis for reclaiming viable social relations, at the same time as resist-

ing the incursions of chaos brought on by "twentieth-century home-lessness." Rather than surplus labour being pumped out of humans, leaving them in a devitalized and vulnerable state, the "reconstitution of society and political authority," as it applies to environmental problems, requires the self-conscious resistance and challenge to capitalist relations.

NOTES

1   This is central to my argument in *Nature and the Crisis of Modernity* (1994).

2   Three of these books include: Martin Lewis' *Green Delusions* (1994), Wallace Kaufman's *No Turning Back* (1994), and Charles Rubin's *The Green Crusade* (1994). I reviewed them in the journal *Capitalism Nature Socialism,* Vol. 6, No. 3, 1995, pp. 117–34.

3   Josef Breuer and Sigmund Freud. 1991. *Studies in Hysteria.* Harmondsworth: Penguin, p. 346.

4   Aihwa Ong. 1987. *Spirits of Resistance and Capitalist Discipline.* Albany: State University of New York Press.

5   Ong. (1987:205).

6   Mark S. Micale. 1995. *Approaching Hysteria: Disease and Its Interpretations.* Princeton: Princeton University Press.

7   Roy Porter quoted in Elaine Showalter. 1997. *Hystories: Hysterical Epidemics and Modern Media.* New York: Columbia University Press, p. 7.

8   Ernest Becker. 1969. "Paranoia: The Poetics of the Human Condition." In *Angel in Armour: A Post Freudian Perspective on the Nature of Man.* New York: George Braziller, pp. 121–55.

9   David Orr. 1994. "Love It or Lose It: The Coming Biophilia Revolution," *Orion,* Winter, pp. 8–15.

10   Orr. (1994:9).

11   John Livingston. 1994. *Rogue Primate: An Exploration of Human Domestication.* Toronto: Key Porter Books, p. 111.

12   Ong. (1987:xiii).

13   Iain McGilchrist. 1995. "It's not so much thinking out what to do, it's the doing of it that sticks me," *London Review of Books,* Nov. 2, p. 28.

14   Ong. (1987:5).

15   Louis Sass. 1992. *Madness and Modernism: Insanity in the Light of Modern Art, Literature, and Thought.* New York: Basic Books, p. 363.

16   Sass. (1992:363–64).

17   Elaine Showalter. 1997. *Hystories: Hysterical Epidemics and Modern Media.* New York: Columbia University Press.

18   Micale. (1995:4).
19   Micale. (1995:8).
20   Ong. (1987:3).
21   Ong. (1987:7–8).
22   Ong. (1987:213).
23   Ong. (1987:4).
24   Ong. (1987:4).
25   Ong. (1987:7).
26   Ong. (1987:9).
27   Martha Noel Evans. 1991. *Fits and Starts: A Geneology of Hysteria in Modern France*. Ithaca: Cornell University Press, p. 34.
28   E. E. Evans-Pritchard quoted in E. P. Thompson. 1967. "Time, Work-Discipline, and Industrial Capitalism," *Past and Present*, Vol. 38, Dec., p.58.
29   Thompson. (1967:58–59).
30   Thompson. (1967:78).
31   Karl Polanyi. 1957. *The Great Transformation: The Political and Economic Origins of our Time*. Boston: Beacon Press, p. 40.
32   Polanyi. (1957:42).
33   Thompson. (1967:91).
34   G. K. Chesterton quoted in Becker. (1969:121).
35   Becker. (1969:154).
36   Thompson. (1967:93–94).
37   Thomas Homer-Dixon. 1994. "Environmental Scarcities and Violent Conflict," *International Security*, Vol. 19, No. 1 (Summer), pp. 5–40.
38   Homer-Dixon. (1994:5).
39   Homer-Dixon. (1994:6).
40   Homer-Dixon. (1994:6–7).
41   Homer-Dixon. (1994:9).
42   E. P. Thompson. 1971. "The Moral Economy of the English Crowd in the Eighteenth Century," *Past and Present*, No. 50, February, p. 76.
43   Homer-Dixon. (1994:16–17).
44   Homer-Dixon. (1994:17).
45   Serge Latouche. 1993. *In the Wake of the Affluent Society: An Exploration of Post-Development*. London: Zed Books, p. 223.
46   Paul Richards. 1996. *Fighting For The Rain Forest: War, Youth and Resources in Sierra Leone*. Portsmouth: James Curry and Heineman, p. xiii.
47   Richards. (1996:xiv).
48   Robert Kaplan. 1994. "The Coming Anarchy," *The Atlantic Monthly*, February, pp. 44–77.
49   Richards. (1996:xvii).

50   Richards. (1996:xviii).
51   Richards. (1996:xxix).
52   Stephen Gill. 1995. "Theorizing the Interregnum: The Double Move-
        ment and Global Politics in the 1990s." In *International Political Economy:
        Understanding Global Disorder.* Björn Hettne [Ed.]. Halifax: Fernwood,
        p. 69.
53   Björn Hettne. 1995. "Introduction." In Hettne. (1995:12).
54   Hettne. (1995:12).
55   Robert Cox. 1995. "Critical Political Economy." In Hettne. (1995:37).
56   Cox. (1995:39).
57   Cox. (1995:39,41).
58   Cox. (1995:45).

V

Environmental Policy Making: Resolving Issues or Solving History?

The schizophrenic approach to production and conservation with 'production' being based on uniformity, and 'conservation' desperately attempting to preserve diversity as raw material against the forces of expanding monocultures, guarantees that neither biodiversity nor people's access to it will be protected. They can only be protected by making diversity the **basis** and **foundation** of production and economic activity, not merely an 'input.'

Vandana Shiva[1]

The history of conservation in modern society is very short. Comprehensive approaches to conservation are only three or four decades old. By contrast, the last three or four centuries have been primarily concerned with organizing society around activities concerned with the increased utility and efficiency of economic processes. The purpose of public institutions such as the Department of Forests and the Department of Natural Resources was to facilitate the efficient conversion of resources into commodities and services for the betterment of society. These concerns were seen almost entirely from the economic point of view.

The history of Canada is all but synonymous with the conversion of these "riches" into wealth and jobs for Canadian society. This led to the prominence of the staples theory of the country's history, where the importance of furs, fish, forests, and agriculture have a defining aspect to the make-up of Canada. The same kind of perspective informed government departments. Jurisdictional responsibilities had to do generating economic activity. Whereas economic growth can be supported in an efficient manner through more narrow sectoral approaches, environmental problems are messy in biophysical terms, and therefore also in terms of the jurisdictions they intrude upon, as well as the individuals and groups they affect. The number of aspects that therefore have to be considered when dealing with environmental problems — as opposed to economic growth — expand considerably.

Arthur McEvoy outlines a history of conservation in the American context in which he identifies four different perspectives which he sees as defining the transformation of conservation in the 19th and 20th century. Using the specific example of the California fishery, McEvoy describes laissez-faire approaches to conservation, Progressive Era conservation, "tragedy of the commons" conservation, and an approach based on an interactive theory of nature and culture. In laissez-faire conservation, "lawmakers 'naturalized' — set beyond the realm of the knowable and controllable — not only the ecology of natural resources but also the market forces that disrupted that ecology."[2] Neither ecology nor the market were to be intruded on in any way, as natural processes were beyond the realm of public intervention. This approach suited a limited basis of exploitation and a lack of systematic analysis of the ramifications of that limited exploitation, as well as a general lack of government infrastructure at the time.

In the context of Progressive Era conservation, which emerged early in this century, a more comprehensive and interdependent program based on "impartial scientific expertise, economic efficiency, and centralized planning in the public interest" became associated with the modernization of social and economic institutions:

> Unlike the laissez-faire approach to resource problems, the sustained-yield theory [of the Progressive Era] recognized a systematic relationship between harvesting and resource productivity ... [where] the objective findings of expert scientists would lead automatically to an impartial law that would command instant, absolute obedience from market actors.[3]

Although there was a clearer recognition of the need for public intervention, ecology was understood in reductive terms as dependent only on exploitation, rather than in terms of complex ecological interactions. Similarly, the market remained beyond the realm of resource managers, where "demand, technology, and other variables were factors fishery managers had to cope with, but not variables to be controlled."[4]

As examples of ecological collapse began to appear with more regularity in mid-century, questions were raised about the assumptions which informed Progressive Era conservation. Whereas Progressive conservation "envisioned a powerful central state made up of impartial experts who would command a passive citizenry to obey efficient laws," increasingly it was recognized that lawmaking in regulatory terms "merely duplicated" the market in a different form. Thus, the "new reformers" — generally associated with the "tragedy of the commons" metaphor — argued that over-exploitation had no technical, expert-based solution because it had its origin "in the common property legal regimes in which the industry operated."[5] The solution to conservation problems therefore resided in granting private property rights so that market rationality would restore the long-term self-interest in profitability associated with ecologically-prudent stewardship, a condition that could not be achieved when a resource was owned collectively. Although conservation has shifted perspectives, profit remained the only measure of success, and economic activity remains the window into natural processes.

After 1970, concern was increasingly expressed about whether price and profit were viable bases for assessing ecological health. Maximum Sustainable Yield (MSY) was gradually replaced by Optimum Sustainable Yield (OSY), an assessment which linked ecological, social, and economic information in a more cautious approach to exploitation levels. OSY also reflected the fact that "natural resources are more than passive inputs to economic production" and that there was a benefit to society in leaving fish in the ocean for the future, as opposed to earlier views where this would have been regarded as leaving nature in "unproductive idleness." Along with a more complex understanding of ecological processes beyond economic valuation, after 1970 there also emerged a more complex sense of regulation outside of strict adherence to the authority of the state. Inclusion of participant information, such as environmental impact statements, and community input to decision-making expanded conceptions of authority and regulation beyond the market and the state.

By the 1980s, conservation measures had less to do with accurate biological and economic assessments than with attempting to "keep the various groups off each other's necks, keep people feeling that there is some fairness in the system so that they don't become obstructionists."[6] This re-conceptualization of the goal of conservation in social terms leads to a new understanding of the causes of environmental problems:

> Resource depletion may be more a social problem — evidence of a community's inability to integrate its social order in a self sustaining way — than it is a product of the alienated, self-regarding profit motive ...[7]

McEvoy concludes his discussion by stating that:

> Any explanation of environmental change should account for the mutually constitutive nature of ecology, production, and cognition, the latter at the level of the individuals, which we call ideology, or at the societal level, which in the modern world we call law ... All three elements — ecology, production, and cognition — evolve in tandem, each according to its own particular logic and in response to changes in the other two. To externalize any of the three elements ... is to miss the crucial fact that human life and thought are embedded in each other and together in the non-human world.[8]

What is becoming evident in current environmental discussions is that this tripartite of elements are not interactive and embedded in each other. Rather, production all but defines cognition and ecology, as they inform environmental problems. If I am to relate this contention back to Wood's perspective on capitalism: with the increasing privatization of political and social power in the economy, humans are increasingly understood as sources of labour, and nature is seen as a source of resources. Human resources and natural resources are defined by the forces of production. Production is so dominant in these terms that any interactive conception of the relationship between ecology, production, and cognition is entirely a non-starter. As opposed to the disembedding processes of production, conservation requires the re-embedding of these elements in the social fabric of each other, which would therefore require extrication from production, rather than interaction with it.

The current domination of production is reflected in the profound disjunction between the theory and the practice of conservation, where development is very definitely the active agent, and human resources and natural resources are the "constraints" which has to be dealt with in order to insure continued development. Over the last two decades, theoretical approaches to conservation have become increasingly ambitious in order to overcome this disjunction, encompassing processes which have been variously described as integrated, comprehensive, participatory, interdisciplinary, multi-stakeholder, holistic, biocentric, and ecosystem-based, as McEvoy has discussed. These kinds of initiatives were developed in direct response to the recognition that the causes of environmental problems had become increasingly complex, as had the remedial measures which had to be taken in order to overcome these problems. Rather than directly challenging the forces of production, these conservation initiatives have unwittingly facilitated the incorporation of more and more social processes in the economy, thereby completing the domination of economic development. Flags turning white.

At the same time as these increasingly complex approaches to environmental problems were being developed, what is also clear is that the forces of exploitation which cause environmental problems have become increasingly unbridled in the context of the expansion of privatization, deregulation, and free trade. So as conceptual approaches to dealing with environmental problems become more sophisticated and inclusive, the actual institutional and legal capability to underwrite these expanded mandates is, in fact, shrinking. Hence the disjunction between the theory and practice of conservation, as the world continues to be increasingly organized around the forces of modern economy.

In other words, although it may have seemed for a time that conservation may have been gaining some purchase on the forces of development with these more complex approaches to policy making, the practice of conservation reveals the opposite: development continues to play the tune in the anxious game of musical chairs which orchestrate the dwindling context for conservation in socially-embedded terms.

Unintentional accommodation seems to be the order of the day. This is the history of management frameworks in Canada's East Coast fishery. As every stage in that history, there were new incarnations of conservation strategies. When depletion and dependence arrived at the end of the day, it was clear that these conservation strategies amounted to little more than the intensification of an enclosure movement where those not essential to the rationalization process were marginalized, and marine biotic communities collapsed. The rough echo of stainless steel filleting tables being dragged across the concrete floor of the darkened fish plant to the recycling van is the final triumph of technological advance and economic expansion.

As Wolfgang Sachs has described in the transformation of a resistant and challenging "anti-science" ecology to a management-friendly ecosystem approach to conservation, there is a continual co-option of any challenge, as development increasingly defines the terms of ecology, production, and cognition.[9] This continual failure has transformed conservation from an expanding project which attempted to "resolve issues" by internalizing them in the economy, to one that seems to have to extricate conceptions of nature and human identity from capitalist relation, to "solve history" in other words, in order to be successful.

CONTESTABILITY AND CONSERVATION

The history of modern society arguably began with the expansion of agricultural and mercantile capitalism in 16th and 17th century England. Accompanying the expansion of economic activity, societal frameworks began to institutionalize market economy relations that supported this expansion, a process that intensified during the Industrial Revolution as technological developments led to exponential expansion in economic activity.

Despite various counter-movements which challenged this expansion — such as the right to vote, trade unionism, socialism, and feminism — the institutionalization of the structures which support market economy have continued to present day. Economic globalization is the latest incarnation of the institutionalization of the self-expansion of capital.

Within this historical context, environmental concerns can be seen as another counter-movement that attempts to address some of the negative ramifications of technological change and market mechanisms. In general, the institutions that deal with environmental concerns are the same institutions that historically have been the facilitators of economic growth. In the last thirty years, therefore, institutions that were concerned with economic growth, efficiency, and utility, are now engaged in a project centred on "valuing the non-economic." Whereas economic concerns remain paramount in most sectors of society, environmental policy making focuses on non-economic information related mainly to biophysical processes involving pollution and depletion. This non-economic information provides the benchmarks for measuring the possible negative ramifications of economic activity, rather than promoting efficiency and utility in the theoretically-infinite expansion of carrying capacity.

Therefore government departments struggle to adapt their mandate to deal with environmental problems and the altered expectations of the forestry and fishing industries, as well as the wider environmental movement, which are concerned with the negative consequences of over-exploitation. Many times this project is in conflict with economic growth inside the government department itself, or in the overall government platform.

An early example of the attempt to create a comprehensive global conservation initiative is set out in the *World Conservation Strategy* (1980). The WCS defines conservation as having three objectives: maintaining essential ecological processes and life-support systems; preserving genetic diversity; and sustainable utilization of resources. To fulfill these objectives, the WCS claims that environmental policy must be a multi-stranded initiative which incorporates a strategy for peace, a strategy for a new international economic order, a strategy for human rights, a strategy for overcoming poverty, a world food supply strategy, and a population strategy.[10] What is important to recognize here is that the fulfillment of the biophysical objectives of conservation leads into a complex socio-political project involving a range of other important societal issues. Bruce Mitchell outlines six perspectives which are essential if environmental policy-making objectives are to be fulfilled at the global level:

> These six perspectives — sustainable development, Third World concerns, ideologies, integration, intangibles, uncertainty — are all central in resource management, and deserve explicit attention by resource analysts. The value of resource analysis research is likely to be diminished if these fundamental aspects are not recognized and addressed in our research.[11]

Although, as Mitchell states, the value of policy-making will be diminished if these perspectives are ignored, their inclusion makes for a process that is increasingly unwieldy and convoluted, with many opportunities for conflict and breakdown.

If we take as a starting point that the policy processes are initiated when — as set out in theoretical approaches to the policy cycle — it is recognized that there is a "problem" for which current policy is either non-existent or inadequate, what is clear in the history of environmental policy making is that the perceived "problem" as it relates to capitalism has grown in complexity to the point where it is all but synonymous with the historical process. The recognition of the range of perspectives and conflicts that are present in environmental issues is insufficient in itself, unless these points of view are historically-rooted in power relations. If there is failure in past environmental policy making, it is due, in large part, to the insufficient recognition of this deep historicity.

INTERESTS AND PROCESSES

Whereas sectoral management by various government departments was suited to supporting economic growth, these same institutions have great difficulty dealing with the complexity of resolving environmental issues.

This condition has been referred to as "jurisdictional gridlock," and has created a perspective which acknowledges, as Ron Doering states:

> ... that current government institutional arrangements are wholly inadequate to meet the challenge presented by modern environmental problems. The professional literature abounds with analyses which concludes that present systems of governance (and the "bureaucratic mind") cannot cope with today's global ecological crisis.[12]

Doering goes on to recommend a radical restructuring of the policy process in terms of ecosystem planning, which can take this complexity into account and overcome the narrow sectoral approach of past policy-making. This same kind of recognition is also built into initiatives like integrated resource management, the environmental assessment process, and the multi-stakeholder round-table approach.

The round-table approach to environmental issues — which Canada has played a leading role in developing — is an acknowledgment of this complexity as well as the past failures of government to address it, and an attempt to incorporate the complexity of environmental issues into an information-gathering and decision-making process. The round-table process can create the temporary illusion that those sitting at the table are on a "level playing-field," whereas there is a profound difference is the economic and political power of the participants, and, indeed, the table is tipped at a precipitous angle. When we consider that environmental problems often originate from within the dominant perspectives and priorities of modern society, we are confronted with the perception that these same dominant economic, technological, and scientific realities which inform life in Canada, for example, play a large role in setting the parameters of the way environmental issues are discussed.

These manifold ways of understanding the environment are reflected in the way various perspectives define what is meant by "conservation." Nowhere is this contrast in approaches to environmental issues more apparent and troublesome than in the negotiations between "developed" countries of the Northern Hemisphere and "underdeveloped" countries of the Southern Hemisphere, as regards conservation in the context of such global concerns as population growth, climate change, oceans policy, and deforestation, or with the sustainability debate more generally.

The contrasting ways of defining what "conservation" means in these discussions is a social and cultural debate, as much as it is a economic, technological, and scientific one. Public participation may therefore not only require consultation and interdisciplinary approaches to policy making, it may also require a challenge to the interests and power relations which generated the environmental problem in the first place. The institutions which generated these problems are clearly not the ones who can be expected to resolve them in a significant manner, especially not in favour of those who have less economic and political power. If the current power structures remain in place and define the terms of debate, environmentalism remains a colonial project linked to the intensification of exploitation. If there is to be a "post-colonial" world that has any viability, environmentalism will have to engage in a form of challenge and resistance which "solves" these uneven power relations.

VALUING THE NON-ECONOMIC

With the appearance of more widespread environmental concerns in recent times, conservation approaches have engaged in a project focused on *valuing the non-economic*, as opposed to one that was concerned only with utility and efficiency expressed primarily in economic valuation. The goal of "valuing the non-economic" began as the creation of biophysical benchmarks from which to judge the negative ramifications of certain practices which had in the past been measured only by economic guideposts. "Valuing the non-economic" operates in contrast to, and is circumscribed by, the dominant stream in modernity whereby more and more relations were being rendered in economic terms.

In examining the range of points of view in the current environmental debate, what is clear is that the central issue for conservation is the corresponding characterization of development. Or conversely, in analyzing conservation initiatives the place to start is the examination of how development priorities are presented and the points of negotiation where conservation and development intersect. At one extreme is the complete universalization of development priorities and their permeation of conservation strategies, as illustrated earlier in the work of Panayotou. At the other extreme is the complete problematization of the development project, and the necessity of resistant and challenging strategies of conservation which question the very assumptions of development, as set out in David Orr's terms of biophobia and biophilia. If we think about environmental initiatives as attempting to negotiate a rapprochement between human history and natural history (the evolutionary deep time which created the biosphere), it is possible to characterize these initiatives in terms of the spheres of human history and natural history in which they operate.

At one end of the spectrum, there is the world of environmental economics and resource management which operate entirely within the concerns of human history and make use of the structures and processes of human history. At the other end of the spectrum are the more radical perspectives of deep ecology and biological conservation, which focus on wilderness preservation without regard to present or future human utility, and which define themselves entirely within the biocentric ethos of natural history to the point where the concept of a separate human trajectory is questioned as an impoverished condition which robs humans of their immense legacy in evolution.

The reformist approaches to "valuing the non-economic" operate in terms of biophysical information and regulatory frameworks and focus on what does not fit in the modern economic model. In the fishery, for example, it is common property which is repeatedly identified as the problem, or more generally, it is the externalities which have to be included in the economic equation.

In engaging in this project, attention is paid to the increasing entropy generated in the biosphere through the conversion of low entropy resources into high entropy wastes by the industrial process. In other words, it has to do with the disordering of natural cycles so as to create goods and services, or the disordering of natural history by human history. The environment, as defined in this context, produces resources, absorbs wastes, as well as provides environmental services such as a stable climate.[13]

Environmental policy is therefore concerned with the maintenance of environmental capacity to produce resources, absorb wastes and provide environmental services. Maintaining this capacity or "valuing the non-economic," in these terms is a two-step process: the first step is concerned with biophysical inventory in which environmental capacity is identified. Once it has been identified, the second step is to make use of various instruments whose goal is to bring economic activity within these biophysical parameters. These instruments include such things as voluntary mechanisms, government regulation, government expenditure, and market-based financial incentives. These instruments make use of the various structures and processes of modernity in helping to reform certain activities which cause environmental problems. In these terms, conservation and development have all but identical definitions since they are part of the same structures and processes.

But because environmental problems are becoming increasingly complex in biophysical terms (i.e., in global climate change, automobile use and deforestation are arguably of equal significance), there is a requirement to bring together various jurisdictional responsibilities who have hitherto not been combined. As well as there being increasing complexity in biophysical and jurisdictional terms, there has also been increased participation by environmental groups and community groups who have a direct interest in issues. In the context of a more inclusive and interdisciplinary approach to environmental policy, there is a focus on the relationship between expertise and process, and more broadly, between knowledge and power. Because of the emergence of multi-stakeholder, round-table processes, expert knowledge is confronted with, by definition, an interdisciplinary project in which there is an attempt to link the knowledge of economist, with that of bridge engineers, with biologists etc., in an attempt to create a more comprehensive and integrated environmental policy.

No one knowledge is necessarily prioritized in the interdisciplinary policy process over any other, leading to a consideration that it is not only biophysical information that it is important, but that perspectives from community groups, aboriginal groups and activist organizations must also be included in what is a social as well as biophysical project. These considerations also lead to a recognition that conflicting agendas, and conflicting conceptions of nature and human identity underwrite these decision-making processes, and social issues such as equity now become part of the policy agenda. Theory-practice considerations have to do with these increasingly complex policy processes coming up against vested interests linked to power structures. In other words, the social goals of policy centred on inclusion, equity, and participation come up against the reality that these qualities do not necessarily pervade realities in the larger societal context.

The North-South sustainability debate is an inter-cultural debate which is not just about power, but also has to do with various cultural constructions of social relations and human-nature relations. In international terms, "valuing the non-economic" is not just concerned about differing stakeholder perspectives, but takes on an inter-cultural context. The very use of terms such as "developed" and "developing" countries reflect the ideological aspects of this debate, leading to a situation where different cultural trajectories to that of economic development are categorized in terms that can be described as the "monoculturalization of the other," as the cultural diversity of the South becomes universally defined as insufficiently "developed." Central to the politics of this inter-cultural debate in international environmental policy is the challenge to the privileging of Northern forms of knowledge, and the recognition that, indeed sustainability is as old as the hills, and is not just the goal of a "new calculus" in a reformed modern economy. Environmental policy and conservation in the context of these global concerns would therefore significantly problematize modern economic development as a colonial project which tends not to allow for other cultural trajectories. Michael Redclift has discussed the shortcomings of what he describes as "environmental managerialism" approaches which fail to challenge development priorities in "post-industrial" societies even though they have a fully-developed legal and regulatory infrastructure. This failure is magnified, though, as being an entirely inappropriate approach in what he describes as "structurally-transformed" societies and "small-scale" societies who don't have the rudiments of jurisdictional frameworks which could address environmental concerns in the context of industrial development.[14]

Increasing problematization of industrial production emerges from other cultural trajectories as well as from perspectives rooted in natural history which challenge the one-way mirror of economic development. The challenge to this conceptual separation of human history and natural history — which is, in fact, the reduction of humans and nature as the passive material of development — comes not only from Southern peasant cultures, but also from perspectives in environmental thought and philosophy. In his essay entitled "Ideas of Nature," Raymond Williams states that "Nothing much can be done, nothing much can be even said, until we are able to see the causes of this ... separation of nature and human activity,"[15] as discussed in the introduction. There is therefore a recognition that, many times, there has been an analytical failure which has accompanied ecological failure in environmental policy that has to do with examining the very separation of human history and natural history.

From the perspective of environmental philosophy or the peasant celebration of the "Sacred Grove" in rural India,[16] then, conservation is understood from a biocentric perspective in natural history that is not directly concerned with the present or future utility of nature as it serves human history. This point of view attempts to challenge the priorities of the development project, and highlights a conservation agenda in which "valuing the non-economic" is a biocentric problematization of human history. In these terms, conservation ceases to be a specialty, and is part of the weave of an ethical view of human community and natural community.

What I have set out here are a range of perspectives which inform the attempt to re-integrate human history and natural history. Beginning with reformist environmental policy there is a primary focus of achieving this reckoning through the processes of modern human history. At the other extreme, perspectives on biological conservation operate almost entirely within conceptions of natural history which takes as its starting point the problematization of present or future human utility as regards conservation initiatives. "Valuing the non-economic" moves from biophysical benchmarks and economic instruments in an attempt to internalize the externalities of natural history within human history, to a project I have described as externalizing internalities, where conceptions of human identity and nature are extricated from the modern realities (of human history) in an effort to establish a viable social basis for conservation and human-nature relations within natural history.

An examination of this short history of conservation conveys a sense of transformation in the phrase "valuing the non-economic." It begins as a biophysical concept engaged in by experts, but is gradually transformed into a broader social perspective which concerns itself with consultation, equity issues, and an ethically-based conceptions of nature. In other words, the flag of conservation was initially organized around the idea that economic activity could be strategically altered based on new expert information derived from biophysical data and instituted through law. As it became clear that this approach did not sufficiently challenge economic priorities in modern society, more wide-ranging conceptions of "valuing the non-economic" were developed to not only alter certain economic practices, but to also examine the assumptions upon which economic practices were based. An example of this broad societal approach is conveyed in by Richard Knight and Sarah Bates in *A New Century for Natural Resources Management* in terms where:

> Natural resources management is moving away from simplistic, resource-specific approaches based on scientific, technical "fixes" (thus the theme of recognizing social values in balancing various priorities and making resource decisions) and toward a more integrated, holistic approach that attempts to preserve whole sustainable living systems (thus the theme of broader, biocentric perspectives).[17]

Conservation therefore moved from being a technical project engaged in by experts who operate within the sectoral structures of government departments, to being an inclusive, biocentric process focused on social values. This increasingly complex policy process seemed to be moving from resolving particular issues to the more ambitious project of solving history, in that this process recognizes that significant modern historical realities have to be challenged if environmental policy is to be effective. Central to this recognition is the idea that environmental policy making is inseparable from the social context in which it manifests itself. Or in positive terms, viable environmental policy requires the creation of a viable social context, which in Polanyi terms would require the re-embedding of the economy in society.

The contradiction that these initiatives face is that while the environmental policy process is becoming more inclusive, the corresponding economic and technological realities linked to privatization, deregulation, and free trade — which these increasingly ambitious environmental policy are supposed to address — are becoming less and less accountable to the public sphere. This unintegrated relationship between environmental policy and economic development presents a worthwhile avenue into an analysis of why there is such a disparity between the theory and practice of conservation.

As an "enlightenment project" the multi-stakeholder round-table process of ambitious conservation creates the temporary illusion that those who are gathered around the negotiating table are on an equal footing, and that resolutions of issues can be negotiated among participants with equal access to good information. A Canadian example of this is a report by the *Study Group on Environmental Assessment Hearing Procedures* which states that, in order to fulfill the goal of creating a "harmonious relationship between economic development and environmental protection," the public hearing process will set out:

> the values which the population associates with a specific proposal and as a forum in which expert opinion on technical subjects as well as value judgements or the choices of society may intersect and merge.[18]

As Mary Richardson, Joan Sherman, and Michael Gismondi point out, the theory may set out an enlightenment project, but the practice operates in an entirely different frame of reference:

> There is an inherent power imbalance between project proponents and members of the public in an environmental public hearing. Before a project gets to the stage at which

a public hearing will be held, the proponent must have committed a great deal of money to the project, and secured backing from the government. In the case of the Alpac proposal, the Alberta government that set up the public hearings was the very government that had already given approval in principle to the project, and had agreed to issue debentures and provide support for infrastructure.[19]

What is evident here is that any pretense that the role of government was to promote the "public good" in the name of equity and rule of law has all but evaporated. With the appearance of privatized economic relations in the sphere that used to be occupied by the "sacred trusts" of public responsibility, faith in government has eroded and in this vacuum has appeared what have been called New Social Movements who recognize that this new conflictive arena requires strategic action in the promotion of the group's interests. This broad-based inclusiveness therefore points up the fact that the government has to engage in this kind of approach because it has lost the public's confidence to make policy on its own, as it were. Therefore, many times the consultative policy processes do little more than exacerbate the conflicts that exist in society and render transparent the uneven power relations which the government can no longer mask.

THE "CHRONIC CRUNCH TIME" OF CONSERVATION

At the most simple, level, no one would have paid much attention to an ecological change unless someone with enough power to secure public attention thought they were losing money because of it.

Arthur McEvoy[20]

For conservation and environmental policy to be discussible, they must be problematic. They only become problematic in the context of over-exploitation. The forces which cause this over-exploitation are very powerful. By contrast, the constituency which supports conservation is very weak by comparison. This historical reality does not bode well for conservation.

Therefore, as a specific activity operating in the context of modern industrial society, conservation appears to be all but a lost cause. A consideration of why there seems to be a general failure in the self-conscious practice of the specialty called conservation — with its own processes and regulatory framework — does not have so much to do with the internal details of these practices, but rather with the limited mandate in which conservation operates and the connection between this limited mandate and the powerful economic forces which dominate the larger historical context in which these structures and processes have to participate.

This tension between theory and practice linked to evolving conceptions of the relationship between conservation and development is reflected in the history of the global environmental debate. Beginning with the *Limits to Growth* by Donella and Dennis Meadows, there was the recognition that "if present growth trends in world population, industrialization, pollution, food production, and resource depletion continue unchanged, the limits to growth on this planet will be reached sometime within the next one hundred years."[21] This study was one of the first attempts to use computer modeling to predict future conditions, and although most of their predictions turned out to be incorrect, a debate had been generated about global environmental issues.

This global concern was also reflected in the United Nations Conference on the Human Environment held in Stockholm in 1972, which was the first of a series of environmental initiatives spearheaded by the United Nations, which in turn produced the *World Conservation Strategy* (1980), *Our Common Future* (1987), *Caring for the Earth* (1991), and the Earth Summit in Rio de Janeiro in 1992. There is a concerted tone of "educate and bring on board" approach to global environmentalism in these documents, as if persuasion was seen as the point of entry for dealing with these issues. In *Our Common Future*, this campaign reaches a schizoid and manic crescendo. Chapter after chapter trots out the bleakest of information about energy use or poverty, inevitably ending the discussion with the upbeat "we can do it if we pull together" tone, as if any crack in the enthusiasm will lead to a "no sale." Indeed, after each of these global initiatives, national policy makers returned home with a new map to apply to internal environmental issues, which, in turn produce dutiful government documents quoting the *World Conservation Strategy* or *Our Common Future*, reassuring their constituents that they have "signed on" to the new environmental agenda. These policy makers arrived at the next conference with reports on new initiatives that have been undertaken by their national governments which they can convey to their global compatriots. Meanwhile, the more powerful members of each of these national governments have set about privatizing and deregulating government responsibilities, as these governments not only respond to the global environmental agenda, but also the global economic agenda. Clearly these economic initiatives are the only unified global agenda.

After the failure of the Rio Conference,[22] this evangelical tone in global environmental policy collapsed under its own weight, as well as the weight of industrial interests which scuttled a great many of the initiatives presented at the conference. In the fallout from Rio, a less consistent, less equal, and more competitive debate has emerged in the form of "environmental security" concerns, among others, as I discussed in the previous chapter. Although for a time, United Nations initiatives temporarily recuperated nation-states as viable environmental actors, it is clear now — as it was to those who advocated the inclusion of non-governmental organizations at Rio — that these nation-states are not up to the task of viable environmental policy making in this increasingly "post-Westphalian" world of global economic competitiveness.

This situation leaves environmental policy subject to what could be described as "chronic crunch time." What I mean by "chronic crunch time" is that the goals of conservation are always compromised by the fact that development priorities dominate activities over which conservation is supposed to have jurisdiction, and they do so to the point of the appearance of an environmental problem. Up until this point these activities have taken place as the "normal" activities of society, and there is a complex interweaving of interests and infrastructure which is already in place, and is causing the environmental problem. So the "crunch" comes in two forms. First, it appears that a whole range of societal activities are at odds with conservation measures, with which conservation will then inevitably come into conflict. These measures appear as an awkward obstruction in the metabolism of economic activity, and are therefore resisted not just by the citizens who have jobs or buy products related to these activities, but also the large corporate interests who, in a resource-based economy like Canada's, have considerable sway in the general thrust of government policy.

Second, and in more temporal terms, whereas the theory of conservation moves from analysis and process *toward exploitation*, the practice of conservation proceeds *from over-exploitation*, and is therefore in a constant state of crisis management in which biophysical analysis and policy decisions are cobbled together in an atmosphere of ecological and economic crisis, and where biological information is therefore murky due to over-exploitation, and there is strife and mistrust between stakeholders because conservation appears as a zero-sum game in a situation which is clearly unsustainable.[23] It is for these reasons that conflict and mistrust are endemic to environmental issues.

Modern industrial society operates in the world of unsustainability; or at least, by the time the focus of environmental policy has been brought to bear, the specific issue in question is in the world of unsustainability and the historical forces which brought about the condition of unsustainability are already in place. Therefore, it is necessary to challenge standard practice in a modern economy in order for conservation to be successful. If environmental policy is to promote sustainability, it has to find a way to ratchet down the forces of exploitation which are already in place. Witness the negotiations on global climate change in the fall of 1997 in Kyoto, Japan. As Frank Tester states with regard to Environmental Impact Assessment processes:

> In 36 cases that were subjected to public panel review between the inception of the process in 1973 and January 1992, consideration of underlying development issues was consistently discouraged and most deliberations were focused on the mitigation of negative effects ... Thus while federal assessment reviews have provided a forum for citizen participation, they have not provided an opening for

successful challenges to conventional "development" projects.[24]

It is this gloomy scenario which is illustrated by the case studies set out in the next two chapters on the Pacific Salmon conflict, and on the failed attempt by the Canadian government to pass endangered species protection legislation. Trying to patch up a disaster with a ruin.

In the context of "chronic crunch time," it is all but impossible, then, for the natural world to make an appearance in viable terms, caught as it is in the oncoming headlights of economic development. The paranoid cliff-edge of ecological collapse is not a very promising basis for any kind of reciprocity or symmetry. Everything is stretched to its limit or beyond, including exploitation levels. If there is to be any possibility for an understanding of the natural world which includes humans in a viable way, we are going to have to take a long step back from the cliff-edge. If the line slackens, if the pressure comes off, then there is a possibility for seeing nature as something other than a factory which produces an annual surplus for exploitation. For that to happen, we have to stop seeing ourselves as sources of labour, and for that to happen, there will have to be a questioning of the basic assumptions of modern economic development. On the other side of freezing in the dark lay all kinds of possibilities.

NOTES

1   Vandana Shiva. 1993. *Monocultures of the Mind*. London: Zed Books, p. 44.

2   Arthur McEvoy. 1987. "Toward an Interactive Theory of Nature and Culture: Ecology, Production, and Cognition in the California Fishing Industry," *Environmental Review*, Vol. 11, No. 4, Winter, p. 292.

3   McEvoy. (1987:295).

4   McEvoy. (1987:295).

5   McEvoy. (1987:297).

6   McEvoy. (1987:300).

7   McEvoy. (1987:300).

8   McEvoy. (1987:300–1).

9   Wolfgang Sachs. 1992. "Environment." In *The Development Dictionary*. Wolfgang Sachs [Ed.]. London: Zed Books, pp. 36–39.

10   *World Conservation Strategy.* 1980. "Introduction." Gland: IUCN, UNEP, and WWF.

11   Bruce Mitchell. 1989. *Geography and Resource Analysis.* New York: Longman & Wiley, p. 306.

12   Ronald L. Doering. 1991. *Pathways: Toward an Ecosystem Approach.* Ottawa: Minister of Supply and Services, p. 19.

13   Michael Jacobs. 1993. *The Green Economy: Environment, Sustainable Development, and the Politics of the Future.* Vancouver: University of British Columbia Press, pp. 86–100.

14   Michael Redclift. 1996. "Development and the Environment: Managing the Contradictions." In *Development and Capitalism.* Leslie Sklair [Ed.]. New York: Routledge, pp. 123–39.

15   Raymond Williams. 1980. "Ideas of Nature." In *Problems in Materialism and Culture.* New York: Verso, p. 82.

16   Frédérique Apffel Marglin with Purna Chandra Mishra. 1993. "Sacred Groves: Regenerating the Body, the Land, the Community." In *Global Ecology: A New Arena of Political Conflict.* Wolfgang Sachs [Ed.]. London: Zed Books, pp. 197–207.

17   Richard L. Knight and Sarah F. Bates. 1995. *A New Century for Natural Resources Management.* Washington: Island Press, p. 381.

18   Quoted in Mary Richardson, Joan Sherman and Michael Gismondi. 1993. *Winning Back the Words: Confronting Experts in an Environmental Public Hearing.* Toronto: Garamond Press, p. 9.

19   Richardson, Sherman, and Gismondi. (1993:11).

20   McEvoy. (1987:292).

21   Donella and Dennis Meadows. 1972. *Limits to Growth.* Washington: Potomac Associates. Reprinted in *Green Planet Blues: Environmental Politics from Stockholm to Rio.* Ken Conca, Michael Alberty, and Geoffrey D. Dabelko [Eds.]. Boulder: Westview Press, p. 26.

22   Pratrap Chatterjee and Matthias Finger. 1994. *The Earth Brokers: Power, Politics, and World Development.* New York: Routledge.

23   This is the main argument of my book on Canada's East Coast Fishery: *The Oceans Are Emptying: Fish Wars and Sustainability.* Montreal: Black Rose Books, 1995.

24   Quoted in Richardson, Sherman, and Gismondi. (1993:20).

VI

Prisoners of Their Histories:
Canada/U.S. Conflicts in the Pacific Salmon Fishery

Historians may record more fishery conflicts during one year in the nineties than during the entire nineteenth century.

Lester Brown[1]

During the past three years there has been increasing alarm expressed within sectors of fishing industry in Canada and the United States about the decline in the numbers of salmon entering the rivers of the Pacific Northwest. At the same time, there has been a sharp rise in the number of conflicts and confrontations between the various groups involved in the salmon fishery. This chapter will examine the negotiation process leading up to the signing of the Canada/U.S. Pacific Salmon Treaty of 1985 — and the realities which created the need for such a treaty — as well as assess the success of the Treaty, given the current strife which now dominates the international salmon fishery. Strife is not specific to the Pacific Northwest, but pervades almost all of the world's fisheries. Currently, every ocean fishery is being fished at or beyond capacity. Of the world's fifteen leading ocean fisheries, thirteen of them are in decline.[2] The Pacific salmon fishery provides an evocative case study of the causes of this decline in the world's fisheries, as well as a reflection of the strife which dominates the relationship between participants in the aftermath of ecological collapse, and as such, illustrates what I discussed in the last chapter in terms of the "chronic crunch time" of conservation.

It is my intention, then, to locate the escalating disagreements between Canada and the United States in the Pacific salmon fisheries in terms of the difficulties that confront conservation initiatives and which must deal not only with the difficulties of looming ecological collapse, but also with the collapse of good will and trust in the political and economic context, so that any legal agreement which is struck is immediately confronted with a divisive and hostile group of stakeholders who feel their interests are threatened. Conservation is caught between vulnerable natural processes on the one hand and intransigent economic interests on the other. In sequential terms, what becomes clear in the analysis of the relationship between conservation and development in the case of the Pacific salmon fishery is that conservation is all but ignored in the period preceding the threats of ecological collapse, so conservation initiatives created in the period of looming ecological collapse — such as the Canada/U.S. Pacific Salmon Treaty of 1985 — are insufficient because the standard legal process is superseded by increasing uncertainty in the larger political and economic context. Carl Walters describes this situation in the Canadian Pacific salmon fishery in this way:

> Our historical management approach has produced ... an institutional quagmire, with grossly overcapitalized and bitterly competitive fishing fleets, an allocation system among fishermen that is dominated more by threat of civil disobedience than by reasoned analysis of where rights and privileges ought to lie, and a publicly costly and burdensome apparatus for both biological management and economic support of fishermen ... When (not if) nature deals us a bad hand, through processes such as the decreasing carrying capacity due to climate change, this quagmire will quickly trap any political decision maker who attempts to act wisely on behalf of long term sustainability.[3]

These historical realities, combined with the degradation of salmon habitat resulting from activities outside of the fishery, informs the seeming intractability of the current crisis in Canada/U.S relations in salmon fishery management. This predicament also highlights some of the difficulties which confront the relationship between private and public spheres in modern society. Environmental policy making generally rests on the assumption that publicly-funded bodies operating in the context of the rule of law and equity oversee private individuals and corporations engaged in the competitive production of goods and services. In practice, the line between private and public concerns appears at times to be a porous membrane through which the edicts of economic interests pass. Given the long association between national governments and economic development, governmental institutions have had a very difficult time linking economic activity with ecological realities. In terms of the current difficulties which confront relations between Northern and Southern countries in ongoing environmental discussions, commentators such as Matthias Finger question the viability of nation-states as useful agents in these debates:

> The UNCED-process [United Nations Commission on Environment and Development leading up to the Rio Conference in 1992] has made nation-states managers for global environmental problems, using the process to develop their skills. In the 1970s the nation-states were attacked for not paying enough attention to ecological degradation because they were so focused on development. In fact, they became identified as development agencies. Today, UNCED tries to give them future control over the global environment and rehabilitates them as legitimate actors to deal with the ecological crisis. They [nation-states] in turn will abdicate it to the trans-national corporations (TNCs) as the real engines of industrial growth.[4]

And in a broader sense, it is the intention of this case study to locate this example of Canada/U.S. relations in terms of what Lester Brown describes as the "acceleration of history" which occurs when biological communities are on the brink of collapse. Brown states:

> The pace of change in our world ... threatens to overwhelm the management capacity of political leaders. This acceleration of history comes not only from advancing technology, but also from ... the increasingly frequent collisions

between expanding human demands and the limits of the earth's natural systems.[5]

These historical realities link the crisis in the salmon fishery with a range of environmental problems and their accompanying conflicts. These realities are difficult enough to overcome within national boundaries, but expand greatly when they move to the international context, especially in the North-South debate where cultural assumptions are so profoundly different.

PACIFIC SALMON TREATY OF 1985

> With overharvesting came the need for comprehensive bilateral management to assure a constant, reliable source of salmon for future generations of North America ... It is because salmon are so critical to our economy ... that we must be assured that the economic viability of our fishermen would not be endangered by a treaty with Canada.
>
> Senator Frank Murkowski[6]

The Pacific Salmon Treaty of 1985 required fifteen years of negotiation between Canada and the United States. The far more comprehensive 1985 agreement replaced one of limited scope, dealing only the Fraser River sockeye and pink salmon in a small area of southern British Columbia and Washington State. As well as reflecting the general difficulties in finding ways to limit the expansion of exploitation, the long time-frame required to agree on the terms of the 1985 agreement reflects the challenges involved in dealing with the "interceptions" of migrating schools of salmon by Canadian and American fishers. This problem of "interceptions" has to do with the complex ecological realities of salmon, which includes not only migratory paths in the open ocean, but also their movement up freshwater rivers and streams to spawn. The interface between these complex ecological realities and the political and economic realities of the various interests in the Pacific Northwest — which resulted in Canadian and American fishers catching salmon bound for the other country's rivers — necessitated complex negotiations leading up to the treaty.

The goals of the Pacific Salmon Treaty of 1985 — which has been administered by Pacific Salmon Commission, made up of voting members from Canada, Washington or Oregon, Alaska, and U.S. Native Indian tribes — were to conserve the salmon so that schools could rebuild, to increase enhancement programs, to improve research, and to allocate the catch fairly. International cooperation was seen to be essential to effective fisheries management. Conservation of salmon stocks that migrate across state, tribal, and national boundaries required close coordination among all management entities. Conversely, in the absence of an agreement, conservation and enhancement become much more difficult if only engaged in by individual groups or countries. To take a current example which occurred in the context of the recent breakdown of in Canada/U.S. negotiations, Canada imposed a unilateral ban on commercial and aboriginal harvesting of Stuart sockeye runs because the schools showed signs of depletion in recent years. Disregarding these measures in 1995, the Washington tribes insisted on a harvest of this run of salmon, which Canada opposed. It is this kind of failure at the international level which makes conservation so difficult to achieve, as well as limiting the possibility of the success in investments in various enhancement programs such as habitat restoration, fish ladders, and hatcheries.

The Pacific Salmon Treaty focused on conservation measures in both countries as well as equitable distribution of quotas based on the number of salmon originating from the rivers of each country. This principle of equity — which claims that the economic benefits of the salmon belong to the country of origin of the schools of salmon — was being advocated by Canada and the United States simultaneously in the Pacific Salmon Treaty as well as at the United Nations Third Conference on the Law of the Sea (UNCLOS III). Paragraph 1 of Article 66 in the UNCLOS III document states that: "States in whose rivers anadromous stocks originate shall have the primary interest in and responsibility for such stocks."[7] Although Canada and the United States could readily agree to support this measure in UNCLOS III to curb high seas interceptions of salmon outside their 200-mile limits by other countries, they had a more difficult time sorting out the equity issue between themselves and within their 200-mile limits.

Article III of the Pacific Salmon Treaty sets out the principles of the treaty in this way:

> 1. With respect to stocks subject to this Treaty, each Party shall conduct its fisheries and its salmon enhancement programs so as to:
>
>> (a) prevent overfishing and provide optimum production; and
>>
>> (b) provide for each Party to receive benefits equivalent to the production of salmon originating in its waters.
>
> 2. In fulfilling their obligations pursuant to paragraph 1, the Parties shall cooperate in management, research and enhancement.
>
> 3. In fulfilling their obligations pursuant to paragraph 1, the Parties shall take into account:
>
>> (a) the desirability in most cases of reducing interceptions;
>>
>> (b) the desirability in most cases of avoiding undue disruption of existing fisheries; and
>>
>> (c) annual variations in abundance of the stocks.[8]

At the time the treaty was passed, there was a Memorandum of Understanding attached to the treaty which stated that the equity principle would not be implemented in 1985. The Memorandum also provided guidance on how the equity principle would be implemented when the necessary data on salmon interceptions were developed. Although the parties agreed on interception balances in 1989, the equity principle has yet to be implemented.[9] It was Article III 1(b) which led to the necessity of the Memorandum of Understanding attached to the Treaty because it was this contentious issue which could potentially lead to drastic cuts in levels of exploitation in one country to insure the conservation of fish originating from the rivers of another country. As well as including the

Memorandum of Understanding, the possible threat of lower exploitation levels were mitigated by Article III 3 (b) which states that "undue disruption of existing fisheries" will be avoided. Rather than deal with this divisive issue, it was put off by claiming that more accurate scientific information was required before there could be reliable data on interceptions. As the Memorandum states:

> The principle goals of the Treaty are to enable both countries, through better conservation and enhancement, to increase production of salmon and to ensure that the benefits resulting from each country's efforts accrue to that country. In this regard, research on the migratory movements of stocks subject to interception must be continued for several years.[10]

It is clear from the language used that the main impetus of the negotiations is the prospect of increased exploitation levels (to increase production through conservation and enhancement). The contentious point of interceptions raises the spectre that conservation might actually entail lowering exploitation levels, and it is this prospect that could have been a serious roadblock to an agreement, and was therefore set aside as requiring further research.

The positive wording in the Treaty about conservation and enhancement reflects many of the goals of conservation and sustainability, as set out in a range of documents such as the *World Conservation Strategy, Our Common Future, Caring for the Earth*. The goals of these document focus on ecological and economic stability linked to a biological inventory of the stock. But, as with many conservation documents, the positive approach to conservation belies the history of development imperatives which have undermined conservation and necessitated the creation of such agreements. Conservation documents like the Pacific Salmon Treaty operate in a context of crisis management where ecological considerations become a self-conscious and explicit activity only when development imperatives are threatened. If the theoretical goals of conservation are based on assessing the ecological processes of a particular natural community and setting exploitation levels within the bounds of the generative capacities of those processes, the practice of conservation initiated in a context of crisis yields the opposite results. It is all but impossible to gather reliable ecological data because natural communities are in a state of disequilibrium due to over-exploitation, habitat destruction, as well as fluctuating ocean carrying capacity; and stakeholders resist lowering exploitation in accordance with ecological realities for economic reasons because productive capacity is already in place and is geared to past levels.

The perception of unequal distribution of the catch remains a significant stumbling block to conservation of the salmon, both in international terms, as well as in sectoral terms within the various fisheries in each country. Bud Graham, the Director of Federal fisheries management in British Columbia, states that U.S. interceptions of Canadian fish rose from six million a year in 1985 to nine million in 1994. At the same time, Canadian interception of American fish dropped from 3.5 mil to 2.5 million. Graham believes that equity provisions of the treaty would eventually correct the imbalance, but that hasn't happened: "And in the absence of equity, the incentive to rebuild stocks is low."[11] Echoing this sentiment, a Government of Canada document entitled "The Pacific Salmon Treaty: Conservation and Sharing" states that "Without a Treaty provision for equitable sharing, there is no incentive for one country to conserve, protect and enhance, since the benefits of such actions will flow to fisheries in other countries."[12] Echoing these problems, U.S. negotiator Theodore Kronmiller outlined the difficulties in arriving at the original salmon agreement:

> Despite a fundamental mutuality of interest between the United States and Canada in conservation and enhancement of the Pacific salmon, agreement on a treaty could not be reached for fifteen years. Throughout that period, fishermen on both sides of the border suffered, as many stocks declined, allocations were distorted, and enhancement and research were limited.[13]

Indeed, Canada's boasts about the drop in interceptions by Canadian fishers of American-bound salmon is not necessarily a reflection of a moral stance, but rather, it has resulted from the rapid decline of the Columbia and Snake River coho and chinook, which Canadians had continued to exploit in their waters despite warnings of imminent collapse, in response to Alaskan interceptions of Canadian salmon further north.

The above quotations reverberate with the relentlessness of the logic of over-exploitation in which modern society seems to be imprisoned and which is generally associated with Garrett Hardin's metaphor of "the tragedy of the commons."[14] The "race to fish" which is seen as the central dynamic in the common property "problem" is linked by many practitioners to Hardin's metaphor and is supposed to lead to inefficiency, and over-capacity in the fishery. In other words — these practitioners argue — the fishery will not be fully rational until it has been entirely absorbed within the modern economy model. In an age dominated by movements toward privatization, deregulation and free trade, arguments are made for rationalizing the fishery with measures such as privatizing of fish in the ocean through Individual Transferable Quotas and Enterprise Allocations, and these programs are expanding in virtually every industrial fishery in the world.

Rather than exhibiting the common property "problem," I would argue that over-exploitation is caused by modern economic imperatives and technological capability. It is the relentlessness of Hardin's metaphor which can be linked with Brown's idea of the acceleration of history. The strife, inefficiency, and failure of conservation measures reflects the reality that conservation operates as an "add-on" after development priorities are firmly in place. The limited mandate offered to conservation in dealing with economic and technological realities manages to generate some inefficiencies in exploitation for a time, but generally fails to conserve natural communities. In these terms, ecological crisis is caused by the working out of rational economic behaviour, not by the lack of property rights in the fishery, as is so often argued.[15]

The assumption which underwrote the declaration of the 200-mile limit by coastal states in 1977 was that this move was necessary because past predation by the international distant water fleet which roamed the high seas and collapsed a range of fisheries in the 1960s and 1970s illustrated that a powerful modern fishery required regulation within the circumscribed bounds of the nation-state. Resource managers assumed that scientific analysis and rational management backed by the legal authority of the state could control levels of exploitation, as McEvoy outlined in the previous chapter in terms of the assumptions of Progressive conservation. When this form of comprehensive management increasingly appeared to be a very expensive failure after it was instituted in various forms by nation-states after the 200-mile declarations, arguments were made for privatization of fish quotas as a way to "internalize" regulation within the perspective of exploiters, rather than relying on the "external" regulation of federal fisheries officers. Although these moves tend to concentrate ownership of quota, they do nothing to limit the capacity of the fishing fleet, nor did they promote rational conservation measures. The prospective implementation of these privatizing measures in the Canadian salmon fishery is causing serious conflicts between the small-scale participants in the industry and the Canadian government.

Along with the many current conflicts within the Canada/U.S. Salmon fishery, there were also many external actions which were taken for the sake of development which undermined the viability of the fishery. A long list of development-centred activities took little regard of conservation ramifications: dam construction, urban growth, estuary destruction, raw sewage, industrial effluent, forestry practices such as the logging of headwaters, road building, and agricultural practices near salmon rivers, to name a few. These development priorities have had a profound effect on the health of the runs of salmon in both Canada and the United States so that a great many of them are currently "at a high risk of extinction," as reported in a study by the American Fisheries Society.[16] The recently completed four-year investigation by biologists of the American Fisheries Society identified 142 extinct salmon runs in the province and over 600 at high risk of extinction. Similarly, a 1995 study by biologists working for the Nuu Chah Nulth Tribal Fisheries concluded that 63 per cent of the chinook runs on the west coast of Vancouver Island are at a high risk of extinction. The conflict which is endemic between conservation of salmon habitat and external pressures from ancillary human activity all but matches the destructive activities which was going on within the fishery.

CURRENT CANADA/U.S. CONFLICTS IN THE PACIFIC SALMON FISHERY

> The only way it is going to work is if all parties come back into the treaty process. The more it's outside that process, the less it is likely to succeed.
>
> David Benton, Alaskan Deputy Commissioner[17]

The fishing arrangements for Pacific Salmon Treaty expired three years ago and the deepening ecological and economic crisis has made it difficult to re-negotiate. In the context of this crisis, U.S. fishers started lobbying for a greater share of the catch, as well as intercepting more salmon before they could return to Canadian rivers as Canadian fishers began to benefit from the increased productivity of Canadian stocks. Canada responded by briefly imposing a $1,500 fee on U.S. vessels passing through Canadian waters in the 1994 to punish U.S. fishers, as well as continuing to fish American-bound salmon off the west coast of Vancouver Island that were in a fragile ecological state.

Among the many failures which now confront salmon fishery management, the breakdown of the international policy process in early in 1996 is typical of current problems. After walking away from the bargaining table, the American delegation declared an Alaskan ceiling for chinook that was more than twice that recommended by Canadian biologists. "It's a body blow to the process" said then Revenue Minister David Anderson, later to become Fisheries Minister. "The relationship is not happening as it should."[18] British Columbia Premier Glen Clark presents the kinds of anomalous behaviour which begins to pervade the disintegration of international trust and good will this way:

> It's a travesty. It demonstrates yet again the federal government inaction to deal with the Pacific Salmon Treaty and it's of serious consequences to British Columbians ...

> We have abolished [for this year] the commercial fishery
> for chinook salmon, severely curtailed the sports fishery
> … and at the same time, Alaskans are going to catch Cana-
> dian chinook. It's not acceptable.[19]

In response to these claims, David Benton — Alaska's representative on the Pacific Salmon Commission — replied "We don't agree at all with the claims some of the more boisterous Canadian officials have been making that this will lead to extinction."[20] By contrast Phil Eby, executive director of the B.C. Fisheries Vessel Owners Association claimed: "Canada is taking extraordinary measures to deal with the conservation problem … and here the Alaskans are continuing to thumb their nose at us."[21] On the Canadian side, there are also signs of escalating salvos. Minister of Fisheries at the time, Fred Mifflin had canceled the "catch and release" restrictions on chinook salmon for the 1997 season which he had imposed on sports fishers in 1996, which will in turn allow aboriginal Haida to engage in a food fishery, even when schools are precariously small. Given the murkiness of ecological information produced in the context of collapse, scientific analysis provides a very malleable benchmark for settling such hostile positions. When combined with the lack of trust, there is little upon which to establish a viable starting point for negotiations.

The difficulties of international negotiations is exacerbated by the points of view of sub-national groups who represent various interests within the Canadian and American fishing industries. In return for agreeing in early 1997 to American calls for the separation of northern and southern salmon issues, Canada has garnered an expanded role in the negotiation process for actual participants in the industry. While many applaud this as a step forward, there are increased pressures on salmon quotas among interest groups whose livelihood depends on access to particular numbers of fish. As is true generally in fishery crises over the past decades, the cries for more fish from an economically-threatened industry drowns out the larger conservation issues upon which everyone's future rests. Internal competition for quota in Canada and the U.S. therefore poses one of the most serious impediments to international negotiation.

In Canada, sub-national interests are reflected in the membership on the Pacific Salmon Commission. Bob Wright of Oak Bay Marine was one of the treaty commissioners until he resigned in 1997 over the failure in negotiations. He owns a series of luxury fishing lodges along the coast of British Columbia. His customers fly in from all over the world to fish for salmon in B.C. waters, and he has, obviously, an intense interest in garnering quota for the sports fishery, which has lost money recently in the "catch and release" program imposed in 1996. So while Wright was representing the conservation of the endangered B.C. and U.S. coho at the treaty table for Canada, his customers fish primarily for coho, chinook, and steelhead salmon.

Dennis Brown is another voice at the negotiating table for Canada. Brown is the former Vice President and spokesperson of the United Fishermen and Allied Workers Union, as well as Special Advisor to the B.C. Premier Glen Clark. The union is a strong voice for commercial fishers, fighting for fair prices and a fair share of the catch. As with the sport fishery, commercial fishers have faced some tough economic times lately. The commercial sector is looking forward to a good run of sockeye this year, but its catches are threatened by the fact that the larger seine boats and gillnetters will have a very limited by-catch (unintentional catch) of endangered coho which could shorten the season for them, and threaten jobs and livelihoods.

Pat Chamut, former Regional Director General of the Federal Department of Fisheries and Oceans and now Assistant Deputy Minister of Operations for DFO, is the third Canadian commissioner at the negotiation table. Along with the special negotiator, it is Chamut who is to represent the national interest in fisheries conservation. Alternate commissioners on the Canadian side include Bud Graham of DFO, Bill Valentine of B.C.'s provincial Aboriginal Affairs, Hubert Haldane of the Nisg'a Tribal Council, and Mike Hunter of the Fisheries Council of British Columbia, which represents many of the larger fisheries interests in British Columbia.

While the Canadian panel has a large representation of industrial interests, the American negotiation team is made up of three government officials and one member of an aboriginal group. David Benton is the

Acting Deputy Commissioner for the Alaska Department of Fish and Game, Robert Turner is from the National Marine Fisheries Service, James Pipkin is a "special negotiator from Washington, and Ron Allen is the Tribal Chairman of the Jamestown S'Klallam Tribe. Alternate commissioners are Jev Shelton of the Alaska Gillnetters, Ted Strong of the Columbia River Inter-Tribal Fish Commission, Rollie Schmitten of the National Marine Fisheries Service, and Rollie Rousseau.

Although questions of sovereignty have formed the basis of many of the confrontations between Canada and the U.S.,[22] it is clear that actions taken within Canada and the U.S. by state agencies have worked in conjunction with commercial interests to cause current problems. So while sovereignty is a basis for the international aspects of the debate over the crisis in the fishery, it seems clear that internal actions by nation-states have not been a viable basis for conservation. The international makeup of the Pacific Salmon Commission continues to reflect the close relationship between commercial interests and national regulatory frameworks which have been detrimental to the goals of conservation in the past.

CONCLUSION: MUTUALLY-ASSURED COLLAPSE

> Many individuals caught up in the crisis of the 1990s — the fisheries managers, the utilities executives, the fishermen, the loggers — could be viewed as prisoners of their histories. Nothing was more important, nor more difficult, than that they should awake from the troubled sleep of those histories.
>
> Joseph Cone[23]

Set in the context of conservation strategies which negotiate the relationship between environment and development, it is clear that conservation measures in the salmon fisheries were all but non-existent before signs of imminent ecological collapse, and that attempts to implement conservation in the aftermath of collapse are overwhelmed by conflicts in competing sectors within each country, as well as the international conflicts between Canada and the United States. This reality is clearly conveyed in the conflicts over quotas between Canada and the U.S. in the summer of 1996:

> In the latest twist in the Canada-U.S. salmon dispute, the Americans are threatening to fish the weak Fraser River sockeye run this year unless Canada cuts its harvest of coho off the west coast of Vancouver Island.
>
> The dispute raises the spectre of an all-out fish war between Canada and the U.S., with each side unilaterally setting its catch limits this year.
>
> The coho-sockeye disagreement is a direct result of the dispute between Canada and Alaska over chinook salmon. Because the U.S. did not agree to catch fewer chinook in the waters off southeast Alaska, Canada does not want to reduce its harvest of coho. And because Canada is unwilling to cut its coho catch, the U.S. is unwilling to hold off on fishing the Fraser sockeye run, which will likely be closed to the Canadian commercial fishery because of its small size.
>
> The negotiations on coho and sockeye are deadlocked and no meetings of the Joint Pacific salmon Commission are planned. Time is running out for a deal because the coho fishery has already opened and the Fraser run peaks next month.[24]

This kind of divisiveness and breakdown carried on throughout 1996 and into the summer and fall of 1997 with ferry blockades, resignations of negotiators and commissioners, and lawsuits. Failures in negotiation and international posturing continue to plague attempts to control exploitation.

In his book *A Common Fate: Endangered Salmon and the People of the Pacific Northwest*, Joseph Cone links this re-conceptualization of the relationship between environment and development to an awareness of an ecological community of which humans are a part:

> Nurtured, this sense of community might encourage a new
> ethos of responsibility, both to other people and to the
> larger ecological system, of which the human community
> is only a part.[25]

It is possible to regard this conception of human/nature community as a socially-embedded alternative to the production model conceptions which pervade the salmon fishery. Unfortunately, it is this sense of community which is so profoundly at odds with the divisive relationships which dominate the salmon fishery in the throes of looming ecological collapse.

What has made the conflict between Canada and the United States so difficult is that their respective histories of economic development have pursed the dream of prosperity only to be awoken to conservation by the spectre of ecological collapse. The threat of collapse is a defining reality in the various national and international conflicts in the salmon fishery. Indeed, these conflicts only make sense if they are seen in the context of economic peril brought on by declining numbers of fish. These conflicts would be unthinkable otherwise, in the same way that the "Turbot War" between Canada and Spain in the spring of 1995 would be unthinkable if it were not framed by the reality of the ecological collapse of the cod in Canadian waters. It is the barbarism of enclosure within economic and technological realities, rather than the barbarism of those who resist these realities, which clearly cause this conflict and unsustainability.

As conceived in these terms, it seems that conservation must, indeed, not only resolve the conflicts within the fishery, it must also wake those involved from a historical nightmare of the most hectored and strife-ridden kind. In attempting to create a new "sense of community" conservation confronts realities where this is the ingredient that is precisely in short supply. In setting out such a socially-embedded project, conservation must then navigate the troubled waters of its dis-embedded opposite.

NOTES

1   Lester Brown. 1996. "Introduction." *State of the World 1996.* New York: Norton, p. 5.

2   Brown. (1996:5).

3   Carl Walters. 1995. *Fish on the Line: The Future of Pacific Fisheries.*
        Vancouver: The David Suzuki Foundation, pp. 4–5.

4   Matthias Finger. 1993. "Politics of the UNCED Process." In *Global
        Ecology* Wolfgang Sachs [Ed.]. London: Zed Books, p.36.

5   Brown. (1996:1).

6   Frank Murkowski. 1985. Pacific Salmon Treaty Hearing before the Com-
        mittee on Foreign Relations, United States Senate, February 22, 1985.
        Washington: U.S. Government Printing Office, Washington, p. 2.

7   United Nations. 1982. *Convention on the Law of the Sea.* Article 66.

8   Pacific Salmon Treaty of 1985. Treaty Series 1985, No. 7. Queen's Printer
        For Canada, Ottawa, 1988, p.8.

9   Government of Canada. 1996. "The Pacific Salmon Treaty: An Over-
        view," May.

10   Pacific Salmon Treaty of 1985, p. 52.

11   Bud Graham. 1996. Quoted in "B.C. urges flexible fleet-cutback plan" by
        Peter O'Neil, *Vancouver Sun,* April 17, B1.

12   Government of Canada document. 1996. "The Pacific Salmon Treaty:
        Conservation and Sharing," May.

13   Theodore Kronmiller. 1985. Pacific Salmon Treaty Hearing Before the
        Hearing before the Committee on Foreign Relations. Washington: U.S.
        Government Printing Office, p. 23.

14   Garrett Hardin. 1977. "The Tragedy of the Commons." In *Managing the
        Commons.* G. Hardin and J. Baden [Eds.]. San Francisco: Freeman and
        Sons, pp. 17–30.

15   See, for example, a special issue on overfishing in *The Ecologist*, April/
        June 1995 and *The Question of the Commons* Bonnie McCay and James
        Acheson [Eds.]. Tucson: University of Arizona Press, 1987.

16   T. L. Slaney, K.D. Hyatt, T.G. Northcote, and R.J. Fielden. 1996. "South-
        eastern Alaska and BC Salmonid Stocks at Risk." American Fisheries
        Society Publication, November.

17   David Benton. 1996. Quoted in "Canadian jump-start only hope for fish
        pact, Alaskan says" by Larry Pynn, *Vancouver Sun,* April 17, p. B1.

18   David Anderson. 1996. Quoted in "Canada to fight Alaskan refusal to
        minimize chinook harvest" by Mike Crawley, *Vancouver Sun,* June 27,
        A6.

19   Glen Clark. In Crawley. (1996:A6).

20   David Benton. In Crawley. (1996:A6).

21   Phil Eby. 1996. Quoted in "B.C. fishermen get slap in face" by Jim
        Morris, *Winnipeg Free Press,* June 27, A4.

22   Glen Clark claimed that the U. S. fishermen "aren't respecting our sover-
      eignty." Quoted in "Ottawa steps in to caution Clark on U. S. fish fight"
      by Jeff Lee and Peter O'Neil, *Vancouver Sun*, April 20, 1996, A1.

23   Joseph Cone. 1995. *A Common Fate: Endangered Salmon and the People
      of the Pacific Northwest*. New York: Henry Holt, p. 295.

24   Mike Crawley. 1996. "U.S. threatens to fish Fraser River sockeye run,"
      Vancouver Sun, July 17, p. A4.

25   Joseph Cone (1995:295).

VII

Policies of Extinction: The Life and Death of Canada's Endangered Species Legislation (1996–97)

We naturalists are neither threatened nor insulted by unpredictable, uncontrollable nature – that's one of its fasci-
nations — but in our desperate effort to show at any cost
that we too are civilized people, that we are not emotional
but entirely rational and objective, we abrogate that which
of all things is our strength and our joy; we abrogate our
feelings. In so doing, we play willingly and directly into the
hands of instrumental rationality, the same rationality that
sees nature not as an experience of our very selves but as
a human utility, a commodity, an externality. We sacrifice
ourselves — and thus nature — to the very ideology that
is wild nature's most intractable enemy.

John A. Livingston[1]

Beginning in April of 1995, when the Task Force on Federal Endangered Species Conservation composed of representatives from
industry, science, and environmental groups was set up, the Federal Government of Canada initiated an elaborate and wide-ranging consultative process in order to develop a comprehensive program for
endangered species protection which would coordinate the efforts of federal, provincial, and territorial governments, as well as involve those from
industry and local communities. In August of 1995, the Canadian Government released a legislative proposal for endangered species protection
and, after nation-wide hearings and extensive stakeholder input on the
proposal, Bill C-65 (Canada Endangered Species Protection Act) was tabled
in the House of Commons on October 31, 1996 by the Minister of the
Environment, Sergio Marchi.

Despite extensive input from those involved in or potentially affected by endangered species protection, Bill C-65 was hotly-debated after it was tabled in Parliament, leading to many amendments being proposed by witnesses who appeared during the clause-by-clause review of the bill by the Standing Committee on Environment and Sustainable Development. Amid widespread disagreement over the changes to the bill, or lack of them, the amended Bill C-65 died on the order paper of the House of Commons when the federal election was called in June of 1997. Given the contentiousness of the issue and the level of conflict which had occurred, the passing of endangered species legislation by a government heading up to an election appeared to be a no-win situation politically.

If conservation is understood as the strategy which negotiates the relationship between environment and development, endangered species protection is arguably the most difficult conservation issue with which to satisfy the stakeholders involved because, in ecological terms, it is a form of conservation which is most centrally concerned with preserving species and habitat on their own terms and for their own sake, rather than for human utility. Coupled with this ecological reality, the forces which cause species and habitat destruction are not always just related to direct exploitation, but also arise from a myriad of activities which only secondarily cause species and habitat loss. This combination of ecological exigency with regard to the environment on the one hand, and amorphous and interconnected day-to-day human activities which have become normalized in the context of modern development on the other, create a context for conservation in which strategies which address these realities are highly-focused in ecological terms in creating biophysical benchmarks for species and habitat protection, but at the same time, are rife with jurisdictional overlap and stakeholder conflict when it comes to creating policy which will alter the broad range of human activities which adversely affect species and habitat.

In examining the conflicting points of view on the strengths and weaknesses of Canada's much-debated Bill C-65, the spectre of "desperate efforts" in the face of "intractable enemies" referred to above by Canadian naturalist John Livingston appears as an apt characterization of the difficulties in accommodating concerns for endangered species and endangered spaces within the structures and processes of modern industrial society, as well as a general description of conservation strategies which attempt to negotiate the relationship between environment and development.

THE INSTITUTIONAL CONTEXT OF CANADIAN ENVIRONMENTAL POLICY MAKING

The division of jurisdictional powers between the federal government and the provinces was originally set out in the British North America Act of 1867 passed by the British Parliament, the purpose of which was to convert the former colony into the country of Canada. This division of powers had three general features: first, federal leadership in establishing national guidelines and objectives; second, federal-provincial consultation and bargaining to establish regulatory standards; and third, provincial enforcement of regulations.[2] Although this division of powers appeared to work well during the expansionary period of the Canadian economy earlier in the century, this arrangement has been a source of ongoing jurisdictional ambiguity with regard to environmental issues.

As set out in the BNA Act, natural resources were generally meant to be the responsibility of the provinces, as were the jurisdictions over public lands and forests, as well as mines and minerals. Fisheries, aboriginal issues, interprovincial and international transport, along with regulation of trade and commerce, were the exclusive jurisdiction of the Federal Parliament, while agriculture was established with joint jurisdiction. This division of powers was meant to be clear and unequivocal, but in practice, there has been a history of intensifying jurisdictional conflict between federal and provincial governments over who has responsibility with regard to environmental issues.

This situation is in large part due to the fact that economic growth can be supported in these jurisdictional and sectoral terms without a great deal of conflict, and that this "development mentality" is the historical raison d'être of various government departments. Environmental problems, however, are implicitly messy and flow from one jurisdiction to the other and create a new set of issues to which government departments have to respond. So whereas the goal of economic growth which informed a great deal of the relationship between the public and private sectors in the twentieth century in Canada was well-adapted to the sectoral approach, the new reality of environmental problems has generated a whole new set of issues which require coordination and consultation not just between various government departments, but also with regard to various interested stakeholders.

These new pressures on the structures and processes of government — especially in a period when there is significant curtailing of public spending — has created difficulties in monitoring and regulation which have been described as "jurisdictional gridlock"[3] in the Canadian environmental policy process. Although the repatriation of the constitution from Britain to Canada in 1982 redefined some of the federal-provincial roles in the area of commerce and taxation, as well as in the federal ability to trigger environmental assessments, this situation has only become worse throughout the 1990s.

This jurisdictional gridlock has also persisted even after the creation of departments such as Environment Canada whose goal has been — in contrast to the more narrow sectoral departments attached to particular interests — to develop a broad enough mandate so that it can effectively deal with environmental issues. The gridlock has remained because, although the mandate is broad, Environment Canada has to rely on the traditional departments for research and enforcement capability. The split between setting guidelines and enforcing regulations that had caused conflict between federal and provincial departments also informed the relationship between the guideline-setting agenda of Environment Canada, and the enforcement mandates of other federal departments, especially when those departments also have close relationships with powerful commercial interests who might be adversely affected by Environment Canada guidelines. The Environment Department does not have similar commercial support. Instead, it has the support of a coalition of environmental groups, and the silent witnessing of the trees.

The history of Canada is all but identical with resource-based activities such as the fur trade, the cod fishery, the lumber industry, as well as agricultural production. The defining aspect of this history is set out in the staples theory in Canadian political economy. These resource-based activities have moved from the colonial context, in which they first emerged, to the current globalized economic relations which now are a defining reality for Canada. The centrality of this export-based dependence on natural resources for the Canadian economy has put a strong stamp on the way the federal and provincial governments are organized and the way they operate. This history also creates a large community of interests for whom endangered species protection legislation created not only a challenge in terms of institutional organization and accountability, but also in terms of the economic interests who have made Canada the re-source-based exporter it is today.

THE STATE OF SPECIES AND HABITAT IN CANADA

> Conservation biology will succeed to the degree that its theoreticians, practitioners, and users acknowledge the larger context in which they exist ... In many situations conservation biology is a crisis discipline ... [where] the risks of non-action may be greater than the risks of inappropriate action.
>
> Michael Soulé[4]

As of September 1996, there are 276 species considered to be at varying degrees of risk of extinction in Canada.[5] The categories of risk currently used include extinct, extirpated, endangered, threatened, and vulnerable. The list includes 46 birds, 53 mammals, 60 fish, 16 amphibians and reptiles, 1 marine mollusk, 95 plants, and 4 lichens. Since Europeans arrived in what is now Canada, eight animal species have become extinct and eleven species are not found anymore in Canada.

In more specific terms, the area that has the largest concentration of endangered species is the Carolinian region of Southern Ontario, which is densely populated, thereby generating a wide degree of habitat loss and habitat fragmentation in what is a relatively small area in ecological terms. Along with the most dramatic and direct relationship of the over-exploitation of natural resources such as that of the Atlantic codfish on

Canada's East Coast, agricultural activities threaten the Eastern Cougar, insecticide and herbicide use have caused the decline of the Sage Thrasher, over-collecting of specimens has endangered the Eastern Prickly Pear Cactus, the filling in of wetlands for agricultural use has endangered the Small White Lady's Slipper, the Western Prairie White Fringed Orchid is threatened by a loss of pollinators, and the Slender Mouse-Ear Cress is adversely affected by invasive non-native weeds.[6]

As opposed to times past when it was possible to see the direct relation between human exploitation and populations of flora and fauna

> [i]n contemporary Canada, things are no longer so simple. Protecting threatened species entails far more than merely restricting hunting and trapping. Today, the twin perils that are most hazardous to endangered species are habitat destruction and environmental contamination. Each is far more deadly and subtle than the gun or trap, and far more difficult to control.[7]

This habitat destruction has to do mainly with loss of old-growth forests, prairies, wetlands, and undisturbed beaches, or with pollution, as in the case of the indirect toxic contamination of such species as the burrowing owl.

The issue of species and habitat loss first garnered national interest in the *National Wildlife Policy and Program* (1966) which set out the first policy on migratory birds in terms where "every effort will be made to prevent the extinction of any species."[8] In 1973, the *Canada Wildlife Act* broadened the federal involvement across Canada from migratory birds to all wild animals and their habitats where

> ... the minister *may*, in cooperation with one or more provincial governments having an interest therein, take such measures as he deems necessary for the protection of any species of non-domestic animal in danger of extinction. [emphasis added][9]

Unlike the *United States Endangered Species Act of 1973*, in which government officials were obligated to act in response to threats to species survival, the Canadian government's responsibility was discretionary, as quoted above. What the Canadian act did do though was begin to provide some enabling legislation for the federal government to become involved in what had in the past been considered a provincial responsibility.

The first national conference in this regard was a symposium held in 1976 entitled *Canada's Threatened Species and Habitats*, sponsored by the Canadian Nature Federation and the World Wildlife Fund (Canada). The purpose of the conference

> was not to demonstrate the obvious for it was now widely known that there are a growing number of endangered or threatened species in Canada and that critical and unique habitats are disappearing or being altered in ways that make them unsuitable for some forms of life. The objective, generally, was to look at facts, exchange ideas, examine some successful management programs, review government policies and make proposals for corrective action.[10]

The main outcome of this examination of the current state of affairs of species and habitat in Canada in the 1970s was rather daunting:

> Indeed, a recurring theme at the conference was the lack of knowledge of these species and the lack of concern on the part of the general public for them. What *was* so often repeated about such species is that the habitat or the natural environment where they live is threatened in one way or another and this means that the species themselves must surely be threatened or vanishing. But no one can say for certain because few records are available either from the past or today.[11]

This lack of baseline biophysical information on endangered species is reflected in a general government response of "no budgets, no programs, no staff"[12] for initiatives which might help mitigate the threats posed to species and habitats. In one of the concluding papers to the conference entitled "Meeting the Needs of the Future: A Federal Wildlife Perspective," J. A. Keith, one of the national directors of the Canadian Wildlife Service, stated that:

> … we must get our act together on a national scale, somehow the scattered driving forces within both non-government and government organizations need to be brought together to form the most powerful central body we can muster. Only in combination can we possibly hope to be effective against the steamroller of resource exploitation; singly, we have been all too easily flattened.[13]

Over twenty years later, this call for a "powerful central body" remains the goal of endangered species and habitat protection.

One of the outcomes of the concerns expressed at this time about species and habitat was the creation of the Committee on the Status of Endangered Wildlife in Canada (COSEWIC), a joint committee made up of scientists from wildlife conservation agencies of the federal, provincial and territorial governments and three environmental groups: the World Wildlife Fund, the Canadian Nature Federation, and the Canadian Wildlife Federation. Its mandate was to commission assessments on a wide range of species each year, and at an annual meeting, assign an appropriate designation for those species that merit concern.

Since its creation, this list of threatened species compiled by COSEWIC has only grown, with very rare instances of species being removed because of improved prospects for the species. In recognition of this expanding list, government agencies responsible for terrestrial vertebrates established a program entitled *Recovery of Nationally Endangered Wildlife* (RENEW) which would develop recovery plans for these threatened species. Once the plan was approved, appropriate agencies would carry out a coordinated effort in what would have to be new areas of intergovernmental, as well as public-private, cooperation.

In 1989, a comprehensive compendium of the state of Canadian species and habitat entitled *On the Brink: Endangered Species in Canada* was put together as a "landmark publication, the first concerted attempt to inform the public about the impending loss of wildlife in this country."[14] In engaging in an analysis of the plight of various species in Canada, the authors state:

> There is a temptation to embellish the accomplishments [of recovery programs], and to distort the humbling truth: namely, that a recovery scheme is nothing more than a last-ditch struggle to prevent a failure from becoming a permanent disaster. If we are not careful, we may be seduced onto a "recovery treadmill" of actions marked by increasing expense and diminishing effectiveness.[15]

Despite the fact that in a 1996 survey, 92 per cent of Canadians stated their support for endangered species legislation, and believed that the federal government should play a leadership role in that protection,[16] and despite the fact that the list of endangered species continues to expand, a "last-ditch struggle" ensued among various groups who were for and against the passing of federal endangered species legislation.

CANADA'S ENDANGERED SPECIES PROTECTION ACT (BILL C-65)

> A compelling rationale and an effective strategy for protecting endangered species will require recognition that contemporary [endangered species] problems are the result of socioeconomic and political forces.
>
> Stephen R. Kellert[17]

Canada is a signatory of the United Nations Convention for the Protection of Biological Diversity in 1992 in which Canada committed itself to "develop and maintain legislation for the protection and/or regulatory provisions for the protection of threatened species and populations."[18]

Canada also signed the Convention on International Trade in Endangered Species (CITIES) which censures those who trade in endangered species. In order to fulfill these international commitments and also respond to the support for endangered species protection legislation expressed by Canadians, the Canadian government tabled Bill C-65 in the House of Commons on October 31, 1996.

This legislation was meant to firmly establish the legal basis of procedures for analysis and recovery initiatives related to endangered species, and to set the terms of closer links between federal and provincial governments in acting on these new regulations, thereby overcoming what had been perceived as the policy failures of the past. The opening summary to Bill C-65 states:

> The purpose of this enactment is to prevent Canadian wildlife species from becoming extirpated or extinct and to provide for the recovery of those that are extirpated, endangered or threatened as a result of human activity ... It respects Aboriginal and treaty rights and the authority of other federal ministers and provincial governments. It establishes a federal-provincial Canadian Endangered Species Conservation Council to provide overall guidance to national endangered species programs and to assure national coordination.[19]

What is made clear here is that the federal goal of protecting endangered species could only be achieved by advancing a comprehensive nation-wide initiative that did not appear, at the same time, as a power grab by the federal government, and instead consulted widely and relied upon ministries and agencies that in the past had sway in areas concerned with resources and wildlife, and which would be affected by endangered species legislation.

Four provinces have already passed endangered species legislation (Manitoba, New Brunswick, Ontario, and Quebec), but all were seen as being very ineffective. In Quebec, not a single animal has been listed in a process that is left to politicians, while in Ontario, where the act only applies to the direct killing of listed species, only four actions have been taken during the 24 years the act has been in force. A similar lack of enforcement exists in Manitoba and New Brunswick.[20]

In their current form, both COSEWIC and RENEW committees have no legal authority and are subject to financial constraints, new policy directions, and political interference. As the implementing body for remedial measures for species at risk, RENEW has produced only fifteen approved recovery plans for the 276 species listed by COSEWIC. The obvious failure of current structures to make inroads on behalf of endangered species has led to the call for new and more comprehensive and legally-binding legislation. The government states with regard to Bill C-65:

> Non-governmental organizations, the provinces, territories, aboriginal peoples, communities, and international governments, as well as representatives of industry, agriculture, mining, forestry, and fisheries will be involved and will work co-operatively with the Government of Canada. This approach will ensure the integration of environmental and socio-economic concerns.[21]

The act covers species on federally-controlled land or species which are already within Ottawa's jurisdiction under the Fisheries Act or the Migratory Birds Convention Act. Species that cross provincial boundaries are not covered in the act, but it does apply to species that cross international boundaries. This creates jurisdictional responsibility that amounts to 60% of Canadian territory, including the Yukon, Northwest Territories, oceans out to the 200-mile limit, and federal land south of the 60th parallel. Because of these territorial restrictions, only 40% of Canada's endangered species would be covered by this new act, since most of the activities which threaten species and habitat are the result of human activity occurring on provincially-managed or private land.

Previous to proposing the bill, the federal government lobbied for the assurances of all ten provincial governments that they would also pass complimentary legislation to protect species at risk. At a conference of all provincial ministers with interests in endangered species legislation that was held a month previous to tabling the bill in the House of Commons on October 31, the Federal Ministry of the Environment sought agreement on the proposed legislation. Provinces such as Alberta, Ontario, and Quebec were opposed to any strong federal role in endangered species protection because it was viewed as an intrusion into provincial jurisdiction. Nonetheless, a National Accord for the Protection of Species at Risk in Canada was reached at the end of the October 2nd meeting which:

> … commits governments to complimentary legislation and programs to ensure that endangered species are protected throughout Canada; and establishes a Council of Ministers that will provide direction, report on progress and resolve disputes.[22]

Along with coordinating these initiatives between federal, provincial, and territorial levels of government, Environment Canada also had to content with "turf wars" in which other federal departments were concerned about losing authority to the Environment Ministry. In an attempt to reassure these interests, it was proposed that the Minister of the Environment would be responsible for administering the act, in conjunction with the Minister of Fisheries and Oceans and the Minister for Canadian Heritage (Parks), who would have responsibility for different aspects of wildlife management, and would implement endangered species initiatives in these areas.

Although the role of COSEWIC was formalized by Bill C-65, the role of scientific analysis is circumscribed by the fact that the federal cabinet will have to pass an order in council for a species to gain the protection of the act. The categories of listing include extinct, extirpated, endangered, threatened, and vulnerable.[23] Once a species has been listed as endangered, a recovery program is initiated by the RENEW committee within one year; within two years if it is listed as threatened or extirpated; and within three years if it is considered vulnerable. These recovery plans, which only apply to terrestrial vertebrates, are to be developed in collaboration with provinces, territories, and other interested parties. In the act, these categories only apply to species protection. There is no direct and explicit reference to habitat protection, aside from protecting "residences" of species that are listed, although it is strongly inferred in terms of viable recovery plans.

In its attempt to negotiate powers between the separate jurisdictions of government, it is useful to compare Bill C-65 with the United States Endangered Species Act. In terms of the scope of the legislation, the U.S. Act applies to species and habitat across U.S. except where there are cooperative agreements with states, in which case state laws take precedence, while Bill C-65 applies to only species, and only those that are on federal land or come under federal jurisdiction such as aquatic species and migratory birds. In terms of public requests for hearings, under the U.S. Act, any person can nominate a species for listing, while under Bill C-65, people can also nominate species for listing but COSEWIC will make a determination which requires political approval from the government. Under the U.S. Act, automatic prohibitions against disturbance apply to all listed species throughout the country, while Bill C-65 applies prohibitions only on federal land. In terms of recovery plans, the U.S. Act calls for plans to be developed and implemented by the government in cooperation with other agencies, whereas Bill C-65 calls for recovery plans only on federal land, and only for terrestrial vertebrates. Any individual can initiate a civil suit against a party that is deemed to be endangering the survival of a species under the U.S. Act, while Bill C-65 allows for a suit only after a person's request has been evaluated by government, and there are measures that prevent what are called frivolous or vexatious calls for legal suits. Penalties under the U.S. Act range up to $100,000 fines and two years in jail, while under Bill C-65 fines range up to $1 million for corporations, and up to $250,000 for individuals and five years in jail. Whereas under the U.S. Act there are no alternate measures which can be taken in lieu of penalties, under Bill C-65 an accused person can avoid court action by agreeing to perform remedial activities with regard to said threatened species.

Canada's Endangered Species Protection legislation came about through a process which is informed by the long history of division of jurisdictional powers in Canada. The complex consultations, as well as the end-product, reflect the difficulties involved in securing viable endangered species legislation in a period where there is a general movement by government agencies toward privatization, deregulation and free trade which were seen as important for a resource-exporting country like Canada to remain competitive in global terms. Rather than aligning government regulations to suit these increasingly important global realities, endangered species legislation operated outside of this exploitation-based perception of nature and, in a period of general government de-regulation, Bill C-65 risked appearing like a power-grab by federal regulators on behalf of "non-consumptive" concerns related to the natural world. This history became very evident in the amendment process which was undertaken after the Bill C-65 passed through first reading in the House of Commons.

JURISDICTIONS, INTERESTS, AND THE AMENDMENT PROCESS OF BILL C-65

After receiving initial approval following first reading in the House of Commons, Bill C-65 was referred to the Environment and Sustainable Development Committee for a clause by clause review, and where interested parties could make presentations and propose amendments to the bill. It was here that the federal government had to tread the difficult territory of jurisdictional overlap with areas that had hitherto been predominantly the responsibility of the provinces, and of passing regulations which had direct implications for industries which exploited Canadian resources, such as forestry, fishing, mining, and agriculture.

An example of these difficult negotiations, which took place during the amendment process, is conveyed in the discussion of habitat concerns for migratory birds and whether Bill C-65 would expand federal powers beyond those which had operated under the Migratory Bird Act or the Fisheries Act, and which had formed the basis of regulations of the past. An interchange took place at the hearings concerning the phrase "and habitat frequented by such migratory birds" which evokes these jurisdictional concerns about whether Bill C-65 would be going beyond past regulations with regard to protecting habitat:

Mr. Steven Curtis (Associate Director, Canadian Wildlife Service, Department of the Environment): ... article 35 of the migratory bird regulations ... prohibits the deposition of deleterious substances into waters or habitats frequented by migratory birds. That in and of itself doesn't give the authority to protect habitat ...

Mr. H. Ian Rounthwaite (Consultant to the Committee): Mr. Chairman, a number of points can be made about this proposed amendment [concerning the scope of migratory bird habitat regulations in Bill C-65] ... The Fisheries Act protects aquatic species by protecting waters frequented by fish. The proposed subamendment wording in terms of protecting areas frequented by migratory birds simply would bring protection of migratory bird habitat in line with the way in which the federal government has always protected aquatic species ... The Supreme Court of Canada has made it very plain that where a matter falls clearly within the federal government's division of powers, a reasonable regulatory scheme that is necessarily incidental to carry out the pith and substance of the federal head of power is entirely permissible and entirely acceptable. I think that's all this does.

Mr. Forseth (Member of Parliament for New Westminster-Burnaby): I clearly recall from the discussions that the Migratory Bird Act (1994) was somewhat limited in its application to habitat. This is a clear effort to reinforce the jurisdiction that it's expansionary in nature. Either wording, one or the other, I think is asserting a federal authority on habitat that previously was contemplated was not fully functional under the Migratory Birds Convention Act. I suppose the objections came up because some of the provinces objected. I recognize here that there is indeed an expansion of jurisdiction by this whole clause.[24]

As reflected in the above discussion, those involved in the policy process were more concerned with limiting legislative authority than with developing viable endangered species legislation. The conservation policy process was used as an opportunity to protect interests, rather than to develop viable conservation measures.

Among the stakeholders involved in the policy process that made representation before the standing committee, industry associations sought to limit the powers outlined in Bill C-65 in arguing that wildlife was a responsibility of the provinces and territories and not that of the federal government. Resource-based industries expressed concern that individuals could launch investigations on potentially endangered species, ignoring the fact that the appropriate government minister could issue permits to exempt any activity from the act or its regulations. In addition to this loophole intended to relieve the concerns of corporate lobby groups, any suit brought forth by a private citizen against a corporation would not adversely affect any given activity until the investigation was completed.

The forestry sector argued that Bill C-65 would not "effectively integrate socio-economic considerations into the development and implementation of feasible recovery plans."[25] The British Columbia forest industry went so far as to publish an advertisement in a daily Vancouver newspaper claiming that Bill C-65 would result in "the sort of socio-economic hardship and dislocation that the U. S. Endangered Species Act produced in the Pacific Northwest,"[26] referring to the controversial protection granted to the spotted owl. These claims were made despite the fact that Bill C-65 only applies to federal land and, in any case, there is no logging on federal land in British Columbia. In similar fashion to the forestry sector, the agricultural community suggested that current regulations were sufficient and feared the potential ramifications for private landowners and their property rights, along with possible financial losses resulting from these new regulations.

These financial concerns, as well as provincial concerns about jurisdictional encroachment, provided significant roadblocks to expanding the regulatory basis of Bill C-65, despite the fact that the Canadian Bar Association stated that "the federal government clearly has jurisdiction to protect species that cross provincial borders and is the only government in Canada with those powers."[27] With all of these commercial interests, along with their proxies in provincial departments and other federal departments lined up against them, the Environment Ministry had only organizations such as the Canadian Endangered Species Coalition, which represents over 100 environmental groups, as well as concerned private citizens, who were lobbying to strengthen the bill. The Environment Ministry also had the support of the Environment and Sustainable Development Committee, which was made up of elected members and government officials who placed a high priority on environmental issues, and therefore played an advocacy role during the amendment process.

The Canadian Endangered Species Coalition was critical of Bill C-65 because it only applied to federal land and therefore gave no protection to over half of the species at risk and over 80% of the plants at risk. The coalition also was critical of the fact that the bill did not protect habitat, despite the recognition that 80% of species endangerment in Canada was due to habitat loss. The coalition was also critical of the fact that the federal cabinet had to approve the listing of endangered species put forth by COSEWIC. If the Endangered Species Protection Act was to have any hope of stemming the tide of habitat and species loss, the coalition argued that the bill would have to:

> 1) Apply to the full extent of federal jurisdiction, with complimentary legislation from provinces and territories. Federal jurisdiction includes, at a minimum, species on federal lands and waters, species listed under the Migratory Bird Act and the Fisheries Act, and species that range or migrate across international or interprovincial borders. The federal law should provide a safety net for Canada's species at risk while respecting provincial competence to protect and recover species in provincial jurisdiction. Where equivalent provincial regulations are enforced, the federal regulations need not apply.
>
> 2) List species at risk and their critical habitat based on scientific criteria. Broad stakeholder involvement is necessary to identify recovery solutions, but determinations of

a species' status and critical requirements is a matter of conservation biology and must be left to the experts. The federal legislation should require the listing of species designated as being at risk by the Committee on the Status of Endangered Wildlife in Canada (COSEWIC).

3) Automatically prohibit killing, harming, harnessing or taking a listed species or destroying its "home." Limited exemptions to these prohibitions should be clearly defined by law and should be open to public review.

4) Require the preparation of recovery plans for all endangered and threatened species within three years of listing. Timely implementation of these plans must be required by law.

5) Require protection of critical habitat of endangered and threatened species, either through automatic prohibitions against habitat destruction or through the implementation of recovery plans that include measures to protect critical habitat.

6) Require the advance review of projects which may adversely affect the protection or recovery of an endangered or threatened species or its critical habitat. Advance review is a cost-effective approach designed to stop problems before they start.[28]

As stated, the Environment and Sustainable Development Committee took on an strong advocacy role during the amendment process because its members believed that the government was behind the bill and would take the political heat caused by a strengthened bill. The committee therefore heeded the concerns such as those raised by the Canadian Endangered Species Coalition and, and as a result, Bill C-65 emerged from the amendment process stronger in several key areas, including the compulsory implementation of recovery plans, the protection of "residences" of species of risk not just on federal land, but in all of Canada, and the expansion of the concept "residences" to include breeding and rearing areas of migratory species such as fish and caribou.

On March 3, 1997, the Standing Committee on Environment and Sustainable Development reported back to Parliament with the amended Bill C-65. Following the bill's return to Parliament, 115 amendments were proposed by Members of Parliament. Forty of these proposed amendments were made by the Minister of the Environment. Most of the amendments undermined the strengthening of regulations that were proposed during the hearing process by reinforcing the primacy of socio-economic interests which may be unduly affected by protection of species at risk. Debate on the bill was stalled for seven weeks, and there was only a token effort to introduce the Bill C-65 on April 24, 1997, before it quickly died on the order paper when the election was called shortly afterwards.

For a government heading into an election, the passing of the endangered species legislation appeared to be a no-win situation. The Federal Department of Fisheries and Oceans (DFO) — one of the main opponents to strong endangered species legislation at the federal level — led the "turf war" because it regarded the legislation as jurisdictional "claim-jumping" by the Department of the Environment. The last thing DFO wanted was the codfish to be declared an endangered species in Canada, because, if it had to abide by endangered species legislation, DFO argued that this would severely curtail its ability to manage the fishery.

The Liberal government had been criticized by Atlantic Canadians for cutting back on Unemployment Insurance payments for seasonal fishery workers, and the perceived failures of The Atlantic Groundfish Strategy (TAGS) program, which paid compensation and retraining premiums to people in the fishing industry who were adversely affected by the fishing moratorium declared in 1992. This made crucial Liberal seats in Atlantic Canada vulnerable, especially following an orchestrated campaign by DFO to paint an even gloomier prognosis for the fishery if Bill C-65 was passed. When this kind of resistance was combined with challenges from the forestry, mining and agricultural sectors, the Liberals regarded the passing of the bill as too risky in political terms, fearing that the passing of the bill would endanger their majority in Parliament. It is not clear whether the new Liberal government elected in June of 1997 has any intention of reintroducing endangered species legislation in the new sitting of Parliament.

AT THE END OF THE DAY: BILL C-65 AS A CASE STUDY IN THE RELATIONSHIP BETWEEN CONSERVATION AND DEVELOPMENT

> In the crunch ... the Ecosphere (nature) ought to be valued above people on the basis of precedence in time, evolutionary creativity and diversity and the complexity of a higher level of organization.
>
> Stan Rowe[29]

In the case of Bill C-65, it is the "socioeconomic and political forces" (to quote Kellert) which were valued "in the crunch" over the "creativity and diversity" of the natural world. In fact, it is possible to claim that almost all conservation policy is plagued with having to operate in a kind of "chronic crunch time" where anthropocentric interests define the terms of the debate, and nature only becomes an issue when these interests are perceived to be threatened. In "crunch time," therefore, it is almost always an economic, rather than an ecological, frame that defines the terms of the discussion. This "chronic crunch time" occurs repeatedly because society is organized around the forces of development, and these forces operate to the point of ecological collapse before conservation action is taken. In the aftermath of collapse, conservation initiatives are begun as a form of crisis management, out of which new policies emerge.

For example, in the case of resource management frameworks in Canada's East Coast fishery or the Pacific Salmon fishery, almost all fishery policy that now exists has emerged out of inquiries into a series of ongoing crises in the fishery.[30] The level of stakeholder conflict which is endemic to the fishery, as well as to other environmental issues, is underwritten by the fact that the forces that cause ecological collapse are already in place, and resist down-sizing since there are so many jobs and so much infrastructure at stake. So, although a situation may be clearly untenable in terms of exploitation or pollution levels, environmental policy initiatives fail in most cases because the forces of unsustainability have sufficient claims on the "well-being" of society, however short-term, over long-term ecological health.

It is this "chronic crunch time" which also creates a context for conservation biology to operate as a "crisis discipline." These are the "desperate efforts" by conservationists referred to by Livingston in the opening quotation where, in their attempt to acknowledge the crisis situation affecting the human interests involved, conservationists end up accommodating the economic frame of reference that is promoting unsustainability. The recognition that standard practice in a modern economy is destroying the natural world is obscured by the attempts by conservationists to placate those whose livelihoods are threatened by unsustainable exploitation of nature, and in doing so, do the important dirty work of development by converting what has in the past between outside of the economic paradigm into terms that is acceptable to that paradigm. Wounded nature and wounded economic interests are sent forth into the fray. This "front-line" of conservation ends up serving the "intractable enemies" of conservation.

Over the last two decades, there have been increasingly ambitious theoretical conceptions of the conservation process: moving from the narrow sectoral approaches which treats conservation as technical issues engaged with by "experts," to a broad inclusive approach which includes a range of stakeholders. In terms of the complexity of the policy process, Bill C-65 seemed to undergo this "integrated, holistic approach." But what appeared as a policy process which was inclusive and which consulted widely in order to promote conservation of endangered species, expressed instead the trepidation of a government who was afraid to overstep its jurisdiction and offend interests on which it was dependent politically. At the end of the day, the Canadian Government was not as interested in developing new conservation legislation for endangered species, as it was in protecting the development interests of a resource-based economy, and the broad range of activities which informed life in an industrial society generally.

Rather than overcoming "jurisdictional gridlock," the inclusive policy process of Bill C-65 gave ample opportunity for powerful economic interests to make their presence felt. As is clear in the case of Bill C-65, the inclusive approach cannot overcome the powerful interests that are present in Canadian society. Downstream conservation has a very difficult time swimming against this powerful current. If conservation is to move up-stream, it will have to challenge the basis of industrial production, and do it before the "crunch time" of species endangerment or ecological col-lapse, when the blood on the floor which draws everyone's attention always seems to be human, rather than that of other sentient beings.

> Things that wash up
> I live in.
> Old dead reeds
> wash up
> at the edge
> of the lake.
> I curl up in them.
> I live in them awhile.

> I can do this.
> I've no fear of this.

> The shells
> that wash up
> in the river.
> No snails in them.
> All cleaned out by the water
> tumbling.
> I live in then awhile.

> Anything
> All things.
> Things that wash up
> I live in.

So now I go walking
with the sounds of water
in my ears.
Little creek sound.
Swift river sound.
The sound of waves on a lake.
I walk toward them.

Oh wash up new things
for me to live in![31]

NOTES

1 John A. Livingston. 1979. "One Man's Celebration," *Ontario Naturalist*, Vol. 19, p. 13.

2 Grace Skogstad and Paul Kopas. 1992. "Environmental Policy in a Federal System: Ottawa and the Provinces." In *Canadian Environmental Policy: Ecosystems, Politics, and Process*. Robert Boardman [Ed.]. Toronto: Oxford University Press, p. 44.

3 Ron Doering. 1991. *Pathways: Toward an Ecosystem Approach*. Foreword to the Interim Report No. 11 for the Royal Commission of the Future of the Toronto Waterfront. Ottawa: Minister of Supply and Services, p. 19.

4 Michael Soulé. 1986. "Conservation Biology and the Real World." In *Conservation Biology: The Science of Scarcity and Diversity*. Michael Soulé [Ed.]. Sunderland: Sinauer Associates, p. 3, 6.

5 See *Committee on the Status of Endangered Wildlife in Canada* (COSEWIC). Environment Canada Webpage, http://www.ec.gc.ca/cws-scf/es/summary_e/intro.htm, (05/14/97,16:41:04).

6 Alex Wellington. 1997. "Endangered Species Policy: Ethics, Politics, Science and Law." In *Canadian Issues in Environmental Ethics*. Alex Wellington, Allan Greebaum, and Wesley Cragg [Eds.]. Peterborough: Broadview Press, p. 200.

7 Canadian Wildlife Service. 1996. "Endangered Species in Canada." Environment Canada. Ottawa: Minister of Supply and Services, Catalogue No. CW69-4/76-1996E.

8 J. A. Keith. 1977. "Meeting the Needs of the Future: A Federal Wildlife Perspective." In *Proceedings of the Symposium on Canada's Threatened Species and Habitats*. Ottawa: Canadian Nature Federation, p. 173.

9   J. A. Keith. (1977:173).

10   Theodore Mosquin. 1977. "Foreword." In *Proceedings of the Symposium on Canada's Threatened Species and Habitats*. Ottawa: Canadian Nature Federation, p. v.

11   Theodore Mosquin. (1977:v).

12   Theodore Mosquin. (1977:vi)

13   J. A. Keith. (1977:174).

14   Candace Savage. 1989. "Foreword." In *On the Brink: Endangered Species in Canada*. J. A. Burnett, C. T. Dauphine Jr., S. H. McCrindle, and T. Mosquin. Saskatoon: Western Producer Prairie Books, p. vii.

15   J. A. Burnett *et al*. (1989:158–59).

16   Canadian Wildlife Service. 1997. "Backgrounder #1: What Protecting Endangered Species Means to Canadians. Environment Canada." Ottawa: Minister of Supply and Services, p. 1.

17   Stephen R. Kellert. 1994. Quoted in *Endangered Species Recovery: Finding the Lessons, Improving the Process*. Tim W. Clark, Richard P. Reading, and Alice L. Clarke [Eds.]. Washington: Island Press, p. 1.

18   Quoted in Wellington (1997:200).

19   Minister of the Environment. 1996. Bill C-65: The House of Commons of Canada, 2nd Session, 35th Parliament. Ottawa: Minister of Supply and Services, p. 1a.

20   Jerry V. DeMarco, Anne C. Bell, and Stuart Elgie. 1997. "The Bear Necessities," *Alternatives Journal*, 23:4, p. 24.

21   Canadian Wildlife Service. 1997. "Overview" of *The Canada Endangered Species Protection Act*. Ottawa: Minister of Supply and Services, March, p. 1.

22   Environment Canada. 1996. Press Release: "Wildlife Ministers Commit to Protecting Canada's Endangered Species," Oct. 2.

23   The Canadian Wildlife Service, Environment Canada defines these terms as follows: extinct species are species that no longer exist; extirpated species no longer exist in the wild in Canada, but they occur elsewhere; endangered species are facing imminent extinction or extirpation; threatened species are likely to become endangered in Canada if limiting factors are not reversed; and vulnerable species are of special concern because of characteristics that make them particularly sensitive to human activities or natural events. "Hinterland Who's Who." Ottawa: Minister of Supply and Services, Catalogue No. CW 69-4/76-1996E.

24   House of Commons. 1997. *Evidence Before Standing Committee on Environment and Sustainable Development*. Chairman: Charles Caccia. Meeting No. 75, Monday, February 17, pp. 12–13.

25   Deborah Gudgeon Harris. 1997. "Federal Act Halted in Parliament," *Recovery: An Endangered Species Newsletter.* Canadian Wildlife Service, Spring, p. 7.

26   Elizabeth May. 1997. "Weak bill can barely protect endangered species," *The Ottawa Citizen*, March 16, A13.

27   Anne McIlroy. 1996. "Environmentalists fear turf war over endangered wildlife," *Toronto Globe and Mail*, October 1, A8.

28   Canadian Endangered Species Coalition. 1997. "Federal Endangered Species Legislation — Background." A bulletin taken from the webpage on Dec. 19, 1997, (http://www.ccn.cs.dal.ca/Environment/FNSN/cesc/bck-su97.html).

29   Stan Rowe. 1990. *Home Place: Essays on Ecology.* Edmonton: NeWest Publishers, p. 125

30   I discuss the fishery at length in *The Oceans Are Emptying: Fish Wars and Sustainability.* Montreal: Black Rose Books, 1995.

31   Howard A. Norman [collector and translator]. 1976. *The Wishing Bone Cycle: Narrative Poems from the Swampy Cree Indians.* New York: Stonehill, p. 100.

Conclusion
Reclaiming the Social Realm:
The Collapse of Canada's East Coast Fishery
and the Politics of Hope

ABDICATION AND AMPUTATION

The central argument of this book is that the "seeming intractability" of environmental problems has to do with the inaccessibility of the forces which cause environmental problems. This inaccessibility has been created by the increasing privatization of political power in the economy, rendering the dynamics of appropriation, and domination beyond the realm of public policy or democratic process. Those who benefit from the internalized political power in the economy do so in private terms, with no sense of public responsibility. In these terms, environmental policy is the public effort to address problems which have resulted from the private accumulation of wealth and power.

This abdication and amputation can be understood as a kind of "double disappearance" where not only is the natural world disappearing in terms of species and habitat, but the human impetus to promote conservation because nature is part of "us" is also disappearing. The fracture of "us" is directly related to the "phantom objectivity" of labour and resources — where humans and nature are the material upon which capital acts — that robs "us" of any of the levers, either experientially or legally, which might begin to address environmental problems.

If this history is to be "solved," a challenge to the forces of capitalism is required. In more specific terms, regarding Canada's East Coast fishery, a democratic project centred around coastal communities is essential if there is to be a challenge to marginalization and ecological collapse. There are measures that can be taken internal to the fishery which can expand economic and political democracy, and which is within the range of activities accessible to fishermen and fish workers. This does not solve the global problems of privatization, deregulation, and free trade which carries on, and which will impinge upon whatever gains are made internally in the fishery. As Ellen Meiksins Wood states:

> Establishing a democratic organization of direct producers ... is in some respects the easy part ... [because] such enterprises would be governed not by the self-determined objectives of those who work in them but by imperatives imposed upon them from without ... by the interests of employers and the coercions imposed by the capitalist market itself: the imperatives of competition, productivity, and profit maximization.[1]

Therefore, what is required are not just barriers to the flow of capital associated with ownership and control — that, afterall, is anathema enough within the current calls for global economic competitiveness — but what is required is "a new driving mechanism, a new rationality, a new economic logic ..."[2] if inequity and over-exploitation are to be challenged.

This search for a "new driving mechanism" is precisely what is not happening in the discussions of new resource management initiatives in the fishery. At the Federal Department of Fisheries and Oceans (DFO) meeting held in Shelburne, Nova Scotia in 1996, a DFO employee made the statement, "We don't care if three boats catch the quota, or if three hundred do." When this claim of "not caring" is combined with the positive statements made about Individual Transferable Quotas (ITQs) as a management approach throughout the meeting, and the continual negative comments about there being too many boats in the fishery, DFO is attempting to sway fishermen toward ITQs as a management approach, as well as discouraging them into leaving the fishery. This is the ongoing refrain of every DFO meeting, and reflects the goal of DFO to privatize the fishery. In this context, ITQs are defined as the privately-held right to harvest a specified tonnage of the Total Allowable Catch from a stock in a given Quota Management Area, which, in turn, will allow for the rationality of the market to exert itself in the fishery.

In Chapter Six, I set out four stages in the evolution conservation identified by Arthur McEvoy as they related to the California fishery, including laissez-faire approaches which regarded the market and ecology as "naturalized forces beyond the realm of analysis," Progressive Era conservation which relied on objective science and rational management to regulate exploitation, "tragedy of the commons" approaches which regarded social issues such as property rights as the cause of environmental problems, and finally, more comprehensive approaches which regarded ecology, production, and cognition as factors which are interdependent. It is this latter stage in conservation which can be related to integrated resource management, ecosystem planning, or round-table multi-stakeholder approaches to conservation. As I have argued throughout this book, this apparently ambitious approach to conservation masks the fact that inclusive processes merely end up allowing for the domination of economic forces over other perspectives which are temporarily given voice at the negotiating table but are shuffled aside in the decision making process.

Therefore conservation merely confirms the hegemony of production as the force which defines both the knowledge of natural processes and the cognitive basis of human perception. Or in the terms I have discussed throughout the book, the domination of market relations pumps surplus labour out of humans and surplus resource out of nature, and conservation strategies seen through the one-way mirror of production merely replicates the process. What this latest stage in conservation amounts to is the abandonment of any concern for equal access to the fishery and the domination of economic relations over social relations. All this is done in the name of efficiency and utility. But how efficient is it to pay 50,000 people to stay home because there are no fish to catch?

Before ITQs completely take over fishery policy in Canada, it is worth examining the experience of countries such as New Zealand who have converted to a privatized management scheme, which have formed the basis of fishery policy there since 1986. In a special issue on overfishing in the journal *The Ecologist*, Leith Duncan assesses the effects of ITQs in the New Zealand fishery in the article entitled "Closed Competition: Fish Quotas in New Zealand."[3] Reflecting the Canadian experience,

Duncan outlines how ITQs were introduced to New Zealand in response to over-exploitation of the fishing grounds and over-capacity in the fishing fleet, as well as the call to lessen the cost of government-funded management programs. As a result of these policies being introduced into the New Zealand fishery, the small-scale inshore fishery has all but disappeared and "corporations now control virtually all fisheries in the countries 200-mile limit" and that "90 per cent of the catch is exported." In turn, Duncan illustrates how conservation measures, allocation of the catch, and enforcement of regulations all experienced major problems under ITQ management. With regard to conservation, the New Zealand government admits that 34 out of the 43 stocks in the fishery are being exploited beyond sustainable limits. The ability to trade by-catches with other boats and lease other quota has created major difficulties in keeping track of catches, and has resulted in the quotas of some species being over-fished by as much as 500% annually. Beyond these legal enforcement problems, there has also been increasing poaching and black marketeering both by license holders as well as by those who lost their entitlement when ITQs were put in place, leading to a situation where up to 80% of the domestic supply of fish for New Zealanders comes through the black market.

When ITQs were first put in place through the use of catch histories in New Zealand, the inshore fishermen were deliberately excluded. The profile of catch histories in New Zealand which were used to establish ITQs showed that 1.3% of the vessels owned by large companies caught 45.2% of the fish, while 2,500 inshore vessels only caught 4.3% of the fish. What is clear here is that any down-sizing in the fleet through the use of catch histories — as became clear in the New Zealand experience — will be done at the expense of the small-boat owners in Atlantic Canada. Also, like the Canadian situation, this was all done in the name of "professionalizing" the industry. What "professionalizing" really means is the corporate take-over of the industry where everyone is an entrepreneur, and therefore the survival of communities need no longer be a concern of fishery policy.

There are remarkable parallels in the history of management in New Zealand and Canada. As Duncan conveys, first there was the establishment of the commercial aspects of the fish stocks which became identified in the annual quota, then there was the identification of who caught that quota, and then there was the granting of a free gift of that share in the form of an ITQ of the quota to the operators who caught it. Therefore, "small-scale operators, and the local people who thought they enjoyed an environmental domain as a collective heritage and a source of sustenance, were told that they did not 'own' it at all." Instead, three large companies own over 60% of the annual quota. Duncan concludes that "the effect upon smaller fishing communities has been serious, and there are very few independent fishermen left in New Zealand." This is clearly an enclosure movement carried out under the guise of conservation.

Obviously, there are severe problems with ITQs as a form of fishery management. The extreme unfairness of the way the quota was divided up, combined with the inability to enforce ITQ catch regulations, resulted in over-exploitation of the fish stocks, and the expanding poaching and black marketeering in New Zealand. As one discouraged fishermen's representative said about the sorry state of the fishery in New Zealand under ITQs, "I never thought I would see the day when I would ever say, 'Get whatever you can out of it. Just don't get caught.' But that is how disgusted I am now."

ITQs are an industry-funded down-sizing strategy which is designed to get the smaller-scale fishermen out of the fishery. Each fisherman — if he qualifies — is given an ITQ that is too small to survive on. He then either has to sell out his share to pay off his debts, or he has to buy out a number of fellow fishermen. There is no lowering of fishing effort in this process, there is only the concentration of it in fewer hands. This is precisely what DFO officials want. Then they can ride around on the yacht of bigwigs in the industry, rather than going to fishery meetings in Shelburne or Yarmouth, and to be yelled at for four hours straight. Fishery policy will be replaced by corporate decision-making. Meanwhile, inshore fishermen will either become wage slaves for one of the larger companies, move on to some other line of work, or they may get disgusted and try to take what they can get, without getting caught, out of the few fish that are left.

The same process of concentration of ownership and marginalization is, of course, not specific to the Atlantic or New Zealand fishery. It is an all but universal feature in the expansion of capitalism. As Gustavo Esteva outlines in his description of Mexican agriculture and its affect on *campesino* peasants, there was a displacement of direct food production and an "integration of direct producers into the sphere of market economy and into the productive logic and accumulation of agribusiness."[4] The political economy of depletion and dependence which defines the enclosure movement in Canada's East Coast fishery is also evident in Mexican agriculture:

> Historical experience indicates that capitalist development in agriculture has taken place in a sort of social vacuum. The *campesinos* have been violently and radically expelled from their lands, for their place to be occupied by other agents. The operation of clearing of estates ... constitute the basis of the model that, with obvious variations, has characterized capitalist expansion in agriculture: in this model ... *campesinos* have no place except as demolition material for constructing the society to which they should incorporate themselves, ceasing to be what they are ...[5]

Given that present choices do not allow them to be who they are, *campesinos*, like fishermen, understand that the economic and social structure in which they have lived until now is falling to pieces, and therefore they find themselves obliged to try their luck in a world still foreign to them. The difficult part — as in all re-education programs — is that they find that this world does not offer them an option for survival and development that has much to do with their own past, which also turns out to be a defining aspect of capitalism. The opaqueness of the commodity versus the transparency of use values.

Although these programs present themselves as a new opportunity, they seem like unattainable goals: there is no economic, social or political space into which direct producers can sign a social contract without, at the same time, agreeing to disappear. Within this conundrum, the only alternative seems to be to construct their own option. In the same way that *campesinos* require a land claim to survive, so do Atlantic fishing communities need a sea claim to secure whatever tenuous hope of survival the ocean might offer:

> What does the *campesino* option mean finally? Land, once again. *Campesinos* already know that having it is not enough, but they also know that nothing is worse than losing it ... They are now beginning to know that not only land should belong to those who work it.
>
> *Campesinos* want freedom through land ... As they cannot and do not always want to answer violence with violence, the *campesinos* have begun to fabricate their own political freedom: to create organizations and areas of negotiation that will enable them to resist the domination they are subjected to, accumulating strength and setting up radical projects of transformation.
>
> Together with political freedom, *campesinos* demand economic freedom ... Economic freedom for *campesinos* means gradually overcoming and eventually eliminating the regulations and organic norms of the economic relations ... through which they are exploited ... Instead of integrating themselves into formal organizations that have converted them and would continue to convert them into modified instruments of domination, *campesinos* demand complete respects for the forms that historically have yielded positive results for them ... [leading to] participation and self-government for effective control of resources ...[6]

Serge Latouche describes "castaways" who suffer a similar fate to *campesinos* or those who live in Atlantic coastal communities:

> Development's castaways also have a double techno-cultural heritage: the residue of their irredeemably lost former identity, and the aborted passage through an inaccessible modernity ... How can the tensions be resolved between

the incompatible cultures, or between the unlimited prom-
ises of the Western dream and the frightful denudation of
harsh reality?[7]

A viable response by the "castaways" requires, in Latouche's terms, "the
economy of reciprocity, with its complex obligations ... [for] which the re-
embedding of the economic within the social effaces any trace of its presence."[8] It is democratic freedom based on "effective control of resources"
and "the re-embedding of the economic within the social" which offers a
politics of hope for Atlantic coastal communities.

THE ATLANTIC GROUNDFISH STRATEGY (TAGS):
A RE-EDUCATION PROGRAM FOR THE NEWLY-STUPID

The past has become talkative, but it is talking nonsense, it
is just playing the fool. For each fact in the present, the
past is giving history ... it is making up astonishing events
and indelible experiences.

J. H. van den Berg[9]

While the larger companies continue to make money by importing
frozen foreign product at low prices for processing, inshore fishermen's
boats and gear rot on the shore. At the same time, these inshore people
are encouraged to leave the fishery through re-training and re-education
programs, while the large companies retain their privatized share of the
fish quota. Enclosure results in the marginalization of those not essential
to increasingly rationalized forms of production.

In terms of the crisis in the fishery and the many other environmental problems we face, what is clear is that modern society is getting
more stupid by the minute. Because it is part of this increasing stupidity,
DFO is unable to promote the conservation of nature, and instead, is the
captive of the economic and technological forces which destroy nature.
As these economic and technological forces have come to dominate the
world, people who live in Atlantic coastal communities or in the Brazilian
rainforest have less and less control over their lives. Those who control

the economic and technological forces want to exploit the resources which these communities have traditionally depended upon, and achieve this by denigrating the way Atlantic coastal communities or native Brazilian communities see the world and talk about it. How do you explain the importance of living in a community and wanting to stay in a community to someone who has never lived in one? Reverse the denigration.

Failures in conservation are informed by two kinds of stupidity:

1) the stupidity of modern society which has lost touch with nature and is destroying it;

2) the coming stupidity of fishermen who have an interactive relationship with nature and depend on it, but have to go and find something else to do because nature is being destroyed, or they no longer have the right to catch the fish that are still out there.

The purpose of resource management as practiced by DFO is to establish the size of the natural resource on which the fishing industry depends, and then to set catch levels that don't overexploit that resource. What the current fishing moratorium has made clear is that DFO has never known how many fish are in the ocean (until now, when there are none), and the current Enterprise Allocation and Individual Transferable Quota program illustrates DFO's intention to turn the resource over to those who are responsible for destroying it. So it has failed on both management goals. The Federal Government has decided to get out of the fish business, and it is going to do it by turning it over the larger companies, and those with the capital reserves to buy up the transferable quotas. In other words, DFO is aggressively pursuing a policy which marginalizes the voice of Atlantic coastal communities.

Think of it now. The fishery collapses, and as part of the TAGS program, you have to go up to Ontario to take your retraining course. Your family is back here. You're living in a dumpy apartment with a couple of fishing buddies who are taking the same course. At first, it's a little bit like a vacation. Lots to see. The Blue Jays are in town. But the school work is harder than you thought. You stick it out for a while, but eventually you give it up. The teacher made you feel like dirt. Your buddies don't like it either, but you can't comfort each other because you've told all the fishing stories three times over, and it only depresses everyone to talk about it anyway. You start drinking more. One night you drink too much and you pass out on the sidewalk. A guy in a suit steps over you and looks down. "Another one of those bloody Atlantic fishermen, I bet. Stupid, and no good for nothing. Worse than the Indians. Must have been born that way."

All the edges you fished along, all the little humps you know, the sense of being part of a world on the ocean, and what's underneath it, all of the knowledge that was passed down to you by older fishermen will be lost. What fishermen have to realize is that this is the important information in the fishery — the located knowledge that comes from inhabiting a place over a long period of time and knowing the comings and goings of the beings that live there with you. This link between located knowledge of a place and a sense of community is a viable basis of conservation that has been practiced in other parts of the world.

DFO has tried to talk you out of that knowledge by claiming that science and management know better. From the declaration of the 200-mile limit onwards, DFO has maintained that resource management regulation is the way to go. But the management practices of DFO have not worked anywhere in the world. All there has been is decimation and destruction wherever you look. What happens is that economic and technological interests come in and make their money by overexploiting the resources of the area, leaving the local communities dependent on handouts, if there are any. So this is the situation you share with communities like your own all over the world: the resource you have depended on is gone, and you start to spend more time worrying about qualifying for handouts than you do about being a fisherman. TAGS is a re-education program for those who are newly-stupid.

So if you accept that DFO knows better than you do, you immediately become stupid because you deny all the knowledge that has existed in communities over generations. Guys in suits with pocket calculators know better than you do what is going on in the ocean. Fisheries officers can insure fairness better than your trust of the fellow you fished alongside of for twenty years. Think about this contrast in your life: you live in a community where the Mountie drives through once a month, and never bothers to slow down. Most of the time you don't have to lock your door, and if something does go missing in the community, you usually know who took it. But whereas life in the community requires almost no regulation, the fishery is one of the most highly-regulated, strife-ridden, and competitive industries in the world. Why is that? The same people participate in both the community and the fishery, but it results in very different behaviour. I would say that the conflict in the fishing industry is the result of the economic and technological forces which are coming to dominate the world and are causing so many of the problems. As is clear in the fishery, regulation as practiced by DFO can't control these forces because conservation of nature requires a recognition of the importance of human communities and their long-term dependence on natural communities. That recognition is disappearing from the world, and that is why we are becoming stupid.

DFO offers no hope. The next time a fishery meeting is called, you would be a lot better off if you turned your back on the stage and started to talk to each other. Solve your own fractured history. In good times, everyone is out for themselves. In bad times, you are better off to look out for each other. Value what you know and care about where you live. No one else does.

Giving oneself over to homesickness and nostalgia are seen as an embarrassing basis for analyzing environmental issues. Radical environmentalists are regularly accused of being nostalgic for a lost unity that never existed in the first place. And yet centuries of history have been driven by the exact opposite: a uni-dimensional pursuit of "progress" and a denigration of everything that was supposedly holding it back.

METAPHORS OF CARE AND MORAL ECONOMY

Metaphor frequently inhabits the margins of discourse and its potential incivility generates concern for its management. Theirs is a subliminal anxiety which results from the difficulty of maintaining the boundary between 'proper'

> terminology in the face of metaphorical boundary-cross-
> ers ... in the sense that certain ideas might not only be out
> of place but out of control.
>
> Gemma Corradi Fiumara[10]

> To take social determination seriously means that one has
> to see oneself and one's shared modes of understanding
> and communication included in that determining. To claim
> otherwise ... is an authoritarian deceit, a magical wonder.
> Those of us who have had to abandon that sort of magic
> are left with ... giving oneself over to a phenomenon rather
> than thinking about it from above.
>
> Michael Taussig[11]

Arthur was upstairs one evening playing cards with his brother Wesley and some friends. It was 1937, later in the fall. He happened to look out the window on the way down the stairs to get a drink of water, and saw a light waving back and forth out on the point. As a fisherman, you get a sick feeling when you see a light where it shouldn't be. Arthur called to the others and they went outside. Sure enough, a light just off the Mad Rocks. They started walking down to the shore and were met by men coming up though the alders: crew from the vessel making for the light they saw from the house. They had rowed across the bay in a dory after the vessel had run aground.

They asked where they were. The crew of the *Douglas and Robert* thought they were heading up into Lockeport Harbour on the other side of the headland. When they knew they were getting close to shore, the skipper had them stop the boat so he could check the depth of water with the sounding lead. Fifteen fathoms. "Let her run for five more minutes and I'll check'er again." He had just come back out on deck and was pulling on his oil pants for the next sounding when she ran aground. That horrible feeling. A beautiful vessel, only three years old, bigger than the *Bluenose* and almost as fast. Three hundred and fifty thousand pounds of salt fish in the hold after over two months out on the banks. Almost to port. Then that terrible heaving up and laying down on her side.

They walked down to the wharf and Arthur started up his boat, as did a couple of the other fishermen. They steamed out to the vessel in the dark and managed to get a couple of tow-ropes aboard, but couldn't budge her. High and dry. "Better wait till morning, when the tide's up," said the skipper still aboard with some of the men. The crew climbed down aboard the boats, except a big Newfoundland dog, who wouldn't leave the boat. He just stood there and barked.

In the slate gray of the morning, it began to breeze up from the east'ard, and with each wave the vessel moved further up onto the rocks, turning sideways in the surf. The boats from harbour could not move her and by nine o'clock it was blowing 30 knots, and the tide had started to fall. The vessel began to break up and salt fish were washing ashore. After being so full of orders, the skipper of the vessel called a halt. "It's no good," he said, dropping the rope he had in his hand. By now, he was the only one left on the boat, except for the dog. The rest of the crew were either in the smaller boats or ashore on the rocks. He took one last turn around the deck, now at a sickening angle. After trying to coax the dog to jump down into the surf, the skipper threw a rope down over the side, lowered himself onto a rock, and waded ashore in the surf.

While only a short time before, they were full of shouts and commands, the crew now stood silent and motionless, looking out. The skipper turned to his mate, and with some deliberateness, said, "If I owned Little Harbour and I owned Hell, I'd rent out Little Harbour and live in Hell."

Throughout the day, it continued to breeze up. Word spread and a crowd had gathered, as had those who had started to scavenge parts of the vessel, as well as the salt cod, which was coming ashore everywhere by now. By evening, it wasn't fit to be outdoors, driving rain and blowing a gale. Those who had kept a lonely vigil out near the vessel could no longer hear or see the dog.

The next morning, the owner of the vessel came down from Lunenburg with a bus to take the crew back. From a distance, you could hear him berating the skipper and the crew as they gathered together with what remained of their kit bags. "Risking it all coming in in the night, just to get one more night of women and drinking."

Where is the place one stands in order to "solve history," outside of the "magic wonder" of the phantom objectivity of capitalism? What is the ground on which one locates oneself to take on the wreck of history? What does it mean to gain perspective by "giving oneself over" to something, rather than observing, as if from above? For the purposes of this book, "giving oneself over" means allowing for the possibility that there is a challenging perspective which can emerge from within those groups which have been dismissed and denigrated in terms of "rebellions of the belly" as described by E. P. Thompson, or as the "vulnerability of being prey" as experienced by Val Plumwood, or as I have described in terms of the "failures of the uninitiated" as related to hysteria in female factory workers, or finally, in terms of re-education and re-location programs for fishermen and fish workers, as set out in The Atlantic Groundfish Strategy (TAGS) in the wake of the collapse of the fishing industry.

I am a re-educated and re-located fisherman. But in the process, I have given myself over to what I have left. To my home near the ocean which now sits empty most of the year. To the boat that I built, which still pounds around on the North Atlantic in whatever short fishing season is left. To my former peers, probably down at the wharf now, leaning on the side of a truck to get out of the wind, someone else down aboard a boat, trading stories.

In a fascist state, the dictator dresses up. He is surrounded by decorum. It all seems so civilized from in there. So with capitalism. For those who have dressed for the occasion, everything seems fine. But from out here, it has a different visage, banal and horrible, at the same time.

Given the route that I have traveled, and the suffering which is currently being experienced by those who begin to sense, six years on, that maybe the fish are not coming back — collapse is a stable state, afterall — analytical questions are also practical questions. A great deal of the environmental debate struggles to imagine alternatives to the intellectual ruin called development. But coastal communities are, to some extent, already outside development because of the collapse of fish communities. They are out in a probationary territory where signs for re-training and re-education are necessary, pointing them back in the direction of "jobs for a new economy."

Most people become involved in environmental issues because they "care" in a world that seems to "not care." It is therefore important to think about the metaphors of care, and the context of "knowing" generally, with which we approach environmental concerns.

The strategic goal of this book is to link the obvious destruction which is occurring at the margins of modern economic development with the less obvious coercion of capitalism which occurs when capitalism is universalized in its centres. Along with the obvious destruction which is going on at the margins — of which the collapse of Canada's East Coast fishery is but one — there is the no less obvious recognition that the cause of this destruction is the intensification of capitalist relations.

Feminist critics have attempted to gain analytical purchase in these terms by examining the relationship between the personal and the larger cultural context as a way of highlighting women's experience in challenging patriarchal domination. Nancy K. Miller regards the use of metaphor as a way to engage in the problematization and challenge of dominant systems. Miller states:

> ... metaphors are to be taken very seriously ... as an economical way both to theorize outside of systems dependent on a unitary signature ... and to imagine in the material of language what hasn't yet come ... into social being.[12]

In the case of capitalism, it is not so much a matter of "what hasn't yet come ... into social being" as it is a case of what has been eradicated from social being by transformations of social relations. What is of importance here is the linking of the obvious cause of the destruction at the tattered edge with the project at capitalism's centre in which it is necessary to find a way to "theorize outside of systems dependent on a unitary signature." Metaphor is important because, as Patricia Yeager states in *Honey-Mad Women*, it provides for a "workaday" access "to extraordinary thinking that we may not yet have tried." Because of their oxymoronic opportunities, metaphors can, as Yeager states, "bring separate spheres of knowledge together, collapsing them into enlightening, encompassing icons."[13]

Marshall Sahlins describes a similar opportunity for challenge when he states:

> Metaphor, analogy, abstraction, specialization: all kinds of semantic improvisations are incident to the everyday enactment of culture, with the chance of becoming general or consensual by their sociological taking up in the going order.[14]

The history of conservation is the history of challenge being taken up by the dominant social order, and rendered ineffectual in the process, which leads Wolfgang Sachs to conclude that "exit roads"[15] from development are becoming increasingly difficult to create.

It is this sense of problematization of dominant structures and an attention to boundary crossing which can be associated with an ethic of care. As Rosemarie Tong states in *Feminine and Feminist Ethics*:

> Care demands no less in the way of integrity, commitment, and heroism than justice. Similarly, rather than dismissing the mother-child relationship as a mindless, thoughtless, "natural" symbiosis, proponents of maternal approaches to ethics have argued that this largely non-voluntary relationship between unequals is a more realistic paradigm for human relationships than the kind of legalistic, formalistic contracts that consenting adults enter into deliberately, consciously, and presumably equally.[16]

Neil Evernden outlines the same sense of denigration in the consideration of human meaning in terms of "fields of care":

> If we were to regard ourselves as 'fields of care' rather than as discrete objects in a neutral environment, our understanding of our relationship to the world might be fundamentally transformed. But to speak of such a transformation is to test the patience of any reader, for it is difficult to take

seriously any claim for the discovery of a new reality. Nor, indeed, is that really what is being required here; rather it is an appeal to remember an old and ever-present reality, something we all experience and yet repress in favour of our cultural beliefs.[17]

It is these conceptions of "care" set out in feminist and environmentalist perspectives which can be related to conceptions of embedded relations, or moral economy, identified in cultures based on reciprocity and redistribution as described by Karl Polanyi.

When the re-embedding of economy in nature is combined with re-embedding the economy in society — a project which arises out of a marginalized group like the Indians in the Chiapas region of Mexico or the Kanak of New Caledonia, as I discussed earlier — then the transformative potential for challenging capitalism greatly increases because there is a located sense of human culture embedded in natural habitat from which to launch this challenge.

In this context, conservation is an all-out challenge to capitalism. In becoming so, conservation disappears as a specialty and instead embeds itself in all aspects of an approach to social relations between humans and between humans and other beings. So in the same way that the autonomous economy disappears into social relations when it is re-embedded, as Polanyi argues, so conservation ceases to operate as a specialty. At their most challenging, embedded economics and conservation can disappear into social relations (What is society for, anyway?). By contrast, capitalism attempts to make human society and nature disappear into the market as labour and resources. Social relations with no economy meets economy with no social relations head-on. The difference that makes a difference.

RADICAL/PRACTICAL CLAIMS FOR ATLANTIC COASTAL COMMUNITIES

To reverse this grim process, which is leading to nothing but social and environmental devastation, we need to iden-

tify the ways corporations and the state have usurped all
aspects of our lives and reestablish viable local communities and participatory democracy.

Edward Goldsmith[18]

If capitalism, then, is concerned with appropriation and expropriation, "solving history" is about re-appropriation, not only of the forces of
production and property centred around market relations, but also of the
significance of social reality and its connection to the natural world. If
capitalism is about the privatization of political power in the economy
where forces of profit and the expansion of capital lead to social and
ecological failure, then "solving history" reverses the domination of economic forces by emancipating humans and nature as viable social actors.
If capitalism is the intrusion of the market relations in the relations between direct producers and their means of subsistence, "solving history"
is about overcoming this dislocation by challenging the re-routing of value
and meaning through the market. The challenge, then, is to set out embedded alternatives which link humans and nature in viable social terms
through the "participation of subjects" rather than the "participation of
objects."

In order to challenge these uneven power relations, sustainability
needs to go beyond the integration of business and government regulation perspectives. In fact, Wood regards both of these alternatives as
futile in themselves:

> ... it seems to me that the main long-term theoretical task
> for the left is to think about alternative mechanisms for
> regulating social production. The old choice between the
> market and central planning is barren.[19]

The "old choice" between the market and government regulation remains
the usual choices available to conservation. As I have argued with regard
to environmental problems, these choices are, indeed, "barren." So here is
the central question for groups such as Atlantic coastal communities:
What are communities to do when market forces have promoted economic

marginalization and depletion of resources, and governments increasingly conceive of their role as supports for those market forces? Every initiative related to the public/private collaboration these days is oriented toward lessening boundaries to the flow of capital and resources in the name of global competitiveness. Local communities such as those on the Atlantic coast have no standing in this world. No community does, human or natural. What is the community which is adapted to global competitiveness? There isn't one. At least not one I want to live in. It was said that Joseph Stalin had a gift for understanding people at their weakest point, and that this was the source of his power. The same is true of capital. It controls people at their weakest point. The hardest thing: make ourselves vulnerable in an increasingly meaner world. A world that doesn't care. Return on investment is a negative interest, a bully's attention:

> On the face of it, capitalism seems to leave very large free spaces outside the economy ... But, in fact, the economy of capitalism has encroached upon and narrowed the extra-economic domain. Capital has gained private control over matters that were once in the public domain, while giving up social and political responsibilities to a formally separate state.[20]

In the case of Atlantic coastal communities, then, the starting point for viable conservation, for whatever fishery is left and for whatever may come back in the future, rests with the strengths internal to the community and external to the market. How does this approach to conservation which begins with the recognition of membership in community present itself as an action plan which challenges the "barren" choices of the market and federal regulation?

> [T]he capitalist market is a *political* as well as an economic space, a terrain not simply of freedom and choice but of domination and coercion. I now want to suggest that *democracy* needs to be reconceived not simply as a political category but as an economic one. What I mean is not sim-

> ply 'economic democracy' as a greater equality of distribu-
> tion. I have in mind democracy as an economic regulator,
> the *driving mechanism* of the economy ... It stands to
> reason that the likeliest place to begin to search for a new
> economic mechanism is at the very base of the economy
> ...[21]

I believe there are three aspects of successful community-based conservation which can begin to provide the basis for this project of creating a
new "driving mechanism," or at least of creating some social space where
it might be considered.[22] The main purpose of such an initiative is to
regain control of market forces by expanding the political domain and
shrinking the private economic power in such a way that public democratic decisions can effectively organize economic institutions such as
property rights and modes of production for catching and processing
fish, and is achieved through community relations:

In full recognition that the Federal Government of Canada laid claim to the
200-mile limit in 1977 because it regarded previous international frameworks as insufficient to protect ecological processes from over-exploitation, Atlantic coastal communities hereby embark on a democratic project
to lay a sea claim to these waters, in full recognition that the Federal
Government regulations are insufficient to protect ecological processes
from over-exploitation. This democratic project of embedded conservation is based on:
1) A Clear Definition of Community — Communities must be clearly defined and have an adequate institutional base to implement its responsibilities. Calls for mere participation, consultation and involvement rarely
incorporates such authority. So institutional capacity has to be created.
There is no point in getting excited about community, if that community
doesn't have a name and an address so that it can assume authority and
be accountable. Community is an ambiguous term, of course, both territo-
rially as well as in terms of membership. A possible definition of community in Atlantic Canada would involve those whose primary relationship
is with the ocean and who interact directly with it. If everyone who could

see the ocean out their window had a say in fishery policy, the industry would be in a lot better shape than it is now.

2) The Establishment of a Hinterland Commons — Without control over the immediate surrounding upon which they depend, community-based approaches are a mere call for involvement, decentralization, and participation which only appears to consult those involved, but leaves the government agency with the authority to do what it wants. Proprietorship by the community allows for the right to determine how and the extent to which a commons is used, rights of access, and rights to benefit from its use. The establishment of a commons allows for the creation of an adequate institutional framework operated by communities. The assumption of proprietorship by communities would require the federal government to give up authority to communities. Right now it is quite happy to give it away through privatization of quotas which exclude communities.

3) Democratic Policy Process — A clear definition of community and the establishment of a commons allows for the creation of a viable conservation process which is democratic and equitable. Conservation can then reflect the long-term interests of communities. This project rests on the assumption that an embedded conservation process can draw on, and at the same time, strengthen the qualities of reciprocity and redistribution within communities as well as their knowledge of, and interest in, conserving marine biotic communities imperpetuity.

Two things occur in this approach to conservation: (1) the space between the conservation organization and the community collapses, so that the community becomes the organization, instead of there being this separation between DFO and coastal communities; and (2) conservation is no longer a special set of objectives pursued on their own separate from all others, but becomes part of a wider set of interests linked to community. In other words, conservation becomes part of a way of living in a community.

What this conservation project recognizes more than anything else is that it is a waste of time trying to second guess what DFO will do next. Coastal communities will have to ask themselves what it is they need to survive, and what kind of world they want to live in, and then set out to lay claim to it, both in social terms as well as in terms of control of the waters they fish.

In *The New Resource Wars*, Al Gedicks describes similar challenges encountered by aboriginal communities who face environmental problems on the one hand and antagonistic governments on the other:

> A common thread running through the case studies of native and rural resistance to ecologically destructive projects is the key role played by native assertion of ... their rights to control the natural resources within their respective territories, the focus of the debate shifted from how this project will be developed, to who will be involved in the decision making process.[23]

From the world of the castaways, where the grip of development slackens, comes a challenge to the forces of appropriation and domination. As Paul Richards claims with regard to a viable future for local communities in Sierra Leone: "They should press ahead with the task of further elaborating local ideas addressing community dilemmas of social integration in their sector of the Atlantic world."[24] In our sector of the Atlantic world a similar project presents itself. As a direct challenge to the ITQ program which marginalizes communities through privatization of fish quota, and the TAGS program which is meant to re-educate the newly-stupid, community conservation resists these incursions and, instead, builds upon the community's stubborn attachment to place, and embedded sense of community. Conservation is not, afterall, an instrumental problem, it is a social project having to do with the participation of subjects.

This transformative social project arises out of what has been left lying around, almost forgotten. As Norman O. Brown states:

> Revisioning as I have experienced it is not a luxury but life itself, a matter of survival; trying to stay alive in history; improvising a raft after shipwreck, out of whatever materials are available.[25]

The materials that are available are the conceptions of humans and nature that require waking from the devitalized condition of labour and resources. The raft is the moral economy which obligates us, one to the other. These materials are currently strewn about the beach, waiting for someone to happen by.

A fellow down the road had a Christmas tree that he had been using for twenty-two years. "Yes, sir. The needles are still on after all these years. Can't believe it."

"Where did you keep it for the rest of the year?"

"Well I just threw it out back in the alders, expecting every year would be the last. The I go out the next year to check before I cut a new one, to see how it looked. Sure enough, the needles were still on."

"How long do you think it'll last?"

"Well, I'm not sure. It's starting to look a little ragged. If I'd know'd it was gonna last this long, I wouldn't have used it so hard."

Nature doesn't mind. It takes such pleasure making new ones.

NOTES

1   Ellen Meiksins Wood. 1995. *Democracy Against Capitalism: Renewing Historical Materialism.* New York: Cambridge University Press, p. 291.
2   Meiksins Wood. (1995:292).
3   Leith Duncan. 1995. "Closed Competition: Fish Quotas in New Zealand." *The Ecologist*, March/June, pp. 97–104.
4   Gustavo Esteva. 1983. *The Struggle for Rural Mexico.* Hadley, Mass.: Bergin & Garvey Publishers, p. 111.
5   Esteva. (1983: 221).
6   Esteva. (1983:231).
7   Serge Latouche. 1993. *In the Wake of the Affluent Society: An Exploration of Post-Development.* London: Zed Books, pp. 215–16.
8   Latouche. (1993:216).
9   J. H. Van den Berg. 1961. *The Changing Nature of Man: Introduction to Historical Psychology.* New York: Norton, p. 135.
10   Gemma Corradi Fiumara. 1995. *The Metaphoric Process: Connections Between Life and Language.* New York: Routledge, p. 3.
11   Michael Taussig. 1992. *The Nervous System.* New York: Routledge, p. 10.

12   Nancy K. Miller. 1991. *Getting Personal: Feminist Occasions and Other Autobiographical Acts*. New York: Routledge, p. xii.

13   Patricia Yeager. 1988. *Honey-Mad Women: Emancipatory Strategies in Women's Writing*. New York: Columbia University Press, p. 33.

14   Marshall Sahlins. 1985. *Islands in History*. Chicago: University of Chicago Press, p. x.

15   Wolfgang Sachs. 1996. "Neo-Development: Global Ecological Management." In *The Case Against the Global Economy and for a Turn Toward the Local*. Jerry Mander and Edward Goldsmith [Eds.]. San Francisco: Sierra Club Books, p. 239–40.

16   Rosemarie Tong. 1993. *Feminine and Feminist Ethics*. Belmont, CA: Wadsworth, p. 225.

17   Neil Evernden. 1985. *Natural Alien: Humankind and Environment*. Toronto: University of Toronto Press, p. 47.

18   Edward Goldsmith. 1996. "The Last Word: Family, Community, Democracy" in Mander and Goldsmith. (1996:501).

19   Meiksins Wood. (1995:289–90).

20   Meiksins Wood. (1995:280).

21   Meiksins Wood. (1995:209–91).

22   For examples of community-based conservation see David Western and R. Michael Wright [Eds.]. 1994. *Natural Connections: Perspectives in Community-based Conservation*. Washington: Island Press.

23   Al Gedicks. 1994. *The New Resource Wars: Native and Environmental Struggles Against Multinational Corporations*. Montreal: Black Rose Books, p. 204.

24   Paul Richards. 1996. *Fighting for the Rainforest: War, Youth and Resources in Sierra Leone*. Portsmouth: James Curry and Heinemann, p. 163.

25   Norman O. Brown. 1991. *Apocalypse and/or Metamorphosis*. Los Angeles: University of California Press, p. 158.

Bibliography

Becker, Ernest. 1969. "Paranoia: The Poetics of the Human Condition." In *Angel in Armour: A Post Freudian Perspective on the Nature of Man.* New York: George Braziller, pp. 121–56.

Beckerman, Wilfred. 1994. "'Sustainable Development': Is it a Useful Concept?," *Environmental Values,* Vol. 3, pp. 191–209.

Breuer, Josef and Sigmund Freud. 1991. *Studies in Hysteria.* Harmondsworth: Penguin.

Brown, Lester. 1996. "Introduction." In *State of the World 1996.* New York: Norton, pp. 3–30.

Brown, Norman O. 1959. *Life Against Death: The Psychoanalytical Meaning of History.* Middletown: Wesleyan University Press.

Brundtland, Gro Harlem. 1987. *Our Common Future.* New York: Oxford University Press.

Canadian Endangered Species Coalition. 1997. "Federal Endangered Species Legislation — Background," *Canadian Endangered Species Coalition Website.* World Wide Website: http://www.ccn.cs.dal.ca /environment/fnsn/cesc/bck-su97.html. December 19.

Canadian Government. 1997. *Evidence Before the Standing Committee on Environment and Sustainable Development.* House of Commons. Meeting No. 75, February 17.

Canadian Government. 1996. *Pacific Salmon Treaty: Conservation and Sharing.* Ottawa: Minister of Supply and Service.

Canadian Government. 1996. *Bill C-65: The House of Commons of Canada, 2nd Session, 35th Parliament.* Ottawa: Minister of Supply and Services.

Canadian Government. 1988. *Pacific Salmon Treaty of 1985. Treaty Series 1985, No. 7.* Ottawa: Queen's Printer.

Canadian Wildlife Service. 1997. *Backgrounder #1: What Protecting Endangered Species Means to Canadians.* Ottawa: Minister of Supply and Services.

Canadian Wildlife Service. 1997. *Overview of the Canada Endangered Species Protection Act.* Ottawa: Minister of Supply and Services.

Canadian Wildlife Service. 1996. *Hinterland Who's Who.* Ottawa: Minister of Supply and Services.

Canadian Wildlife Service. 1996. *Endangered Species in Canada*. Ottawa: Minister of Supply and Services. Catalogue No. CW69-4/76-1996E.

Cassidy, John. 1996. "The Decline of Economics," *The New Yorker,* December 2, pp. 50–51.

Chatterjee, Pratrap and Matthias Finger 1994. *The Earth Brokers: Power, Politics and World Development.* New York: Routledge.

Clark, Tim W., R.P. Reading, and Alice L. Clarke [Eds.]. 1994. *Endangered Species Recovery: Finding the Lessons, Improving the Process.* Washington: Island Press.

Conca, Ken, Michael Alberty, and Geoffrey D. Dabelko. 1995. *Green Planet Blues: Environmental Politics from Stockholm to Rio.* Boulder: Westview Press.

Cone, Joseph. 1995. *A Common Fate: Endangered Salmon and The People of the Pacific Northwest.* New York: Henry Holt.

Cox, Robert. 1995. "Critical Political Economy." In *International Political Economy: Understanding Global Disorder.* Bjorn Hettne [Ed.]. Halifax: Fernwood, pp. 31–45.

Crawley, Mike. 1996. "U.S. threatens to fish Fraser River sockeye run," *Vancouver Sun,* July 17, A4.

Crawley, Mike. 1996. "Canada to fight Alaskan refusal to minimize chinook harvest," *Vancouver Sun,* June 27, A5.

Department of Fisheries and Oceans. 1995. *Lost Stream if the Lower Fraser River.* Ottawa: Minister of Supply and Services.

Doering, Ronald L. 1991. *Pathways: Toward an Ecosytem Approach.* Ottawa: Minister of Supply and Services.

Duncan, Leith. 1995. "Closed Competition: Fish Quotas in New Zealand," *The Ecologist,* Vol. 25, Nos. 2/3, March/June, pp. 97–104.

Environment Canada. 1997. "Committee on the Status of Endangered Wildlife in Canada," *Environment Canada Website.* World Wide Website: http://www.ec.gc.ca/cws-scf/es/summary_e/intro.htm. May 5.

Environment Canada. 1996. *Press Release: Wildlife Ministers Commit to Protecting Canada's Endangered Species.* Ottawa: Environment Canada.

Esteva, Gustavo. 1992. "Development." In *The Development Dictionary.* Wolfgang Sachs [Ed.]. London: Zed Books.

Evans, Martha Noel. 1991. *Fits and Starts: A Genealogy of Hysteria in Modern France.* Ithaca: Cornell University Press.

Ferguson, John. 1996. *What Sustains Sustainability? An Examination of Economic Visions of Sustainability.* PhD Dissertation. Toronto:

Graduate Programme in Social and Political Thought, York University.

Ferenczi, Sandor. 1955. *Final Contributions to the Problems and Methods of Psychoanalytical Meaning of History*. London: Hogarth Press and the Institute of Psychoanalysis.

Finger, Matthias. 1993. "Politics of the UNCED Process." In *Global Ecology*. Wolfgang Sachs [Ed.]. London: Zed Books, pp. 36–48.

Gedicks, Al. 1994. *The New Resource Wars: Native and Environmental Struggles Against Multinational Corporations*. Montreal: Black Rose Books.

Ghai, Dharam and Jessica M. Vivian [Eds.]. 1992. *Grassroots Environmental Action: People's Participation in Sustainable Development*. New York: Routledge.

Gill, Stephen. 1995. "Theorizing the Interregnum: The Double Movement and Global Politics in the 1990s." In *International Political Economy: Understanding Global Disorder*. Bjorn Hettne [Ed.]. Halifax: Fernwood, pp. 65–99.

Gudgeon Harris, Deborah. 1997. "Federal Act Halted in Parliament," *Recovery: An Endangered Species Newsletter*. Canadian Wildlife Service. Spring, p. 7.

Hardin, Garrett. 1977. "The Tragedy of the Commons." In *Managing the Commons*. Garrett Hardin and J. Baden [Eds.]. San Francisco: Freeman and Sons.

Hay, Colin. 1994. "Environmental Security and State Legitimacy." In *Is Capitalism Sustainable? Political Economy and the Politics of Ecology*. Martin O'Connor [Ed.]. New York: Guilford, pp. 217–31.

Hettne, Bjorn. 1995. "Introduction." In *International Political Economy: Understanding Global Disorder*. Halifax: Fernwood, pp. 1–30.

Homer-Dixon, Thomas. 1994. "Environmental Scarcities and Violent Conflict," *International Security,* Vol. 19, No. 1. Summer, pp. 5–40.

Jacobs, Michael. 1993. *The Green Economy: Environment, Sustainable Development and the Politics of the Future*. Vancouver: University of British Colombia Press.

Jones, Norman. 1989. *God and the Moneylenders*. Cambridge: Basil Blackwell.

Kaplan, Robert. 1994. "The Coming Anarchy," *The Atlantic Monthly*. February, pp. 44–77.

Keith, J.A. 1977. "Meeting the Needs of the Future: A Federal Wildlife Perspective." In *Proceedings of the Symposium on Canada's Threatened Species and Habitats*. Theodore Mosquin and Cecile Suchal [Eds.]. Ottawa: Canadian Nature Federation, pp. 173–75.

Knight, Richard L. and Sarah F. Bates. 1995. *A New Century for Natural Resources Management*. Washington: Island Press.

Latouche, Serge. 1993. *In the Wake of the Affluent Society: An Exploration of Post-Exploration*. London: Zed Books.

Lee, Jeff and Peter O'Neil. 1996. "Ottawa steps in to caution Clark on U.S. fish fight," *Vancouver Sun,* April 20, A1.

Livingston, John. 1994. *Rogue Primate: An Exploration of Human Domestication*. Toronto: Key Porter Books.

Livingston, John. 1979. "One Man's Celebration," *Ontario Naturalist,* Vol. 19, p. 13.

Mander, Jerry and Edward Goldsmith [Eds.]. 1996. *The Case Against the Global Economy and for a Turn Toward the Local*. San Francisco: Sierra Club Books.

Marx, Karl. 1971. *Capital III*. Moscow: International Publishers.

May, Elizabeth. 1997. "Weak bill can barely protect endangered species," *The Ottawa Citizen,* March 16, A13.

McCay, Bonnie and James Acheson [Eds.]. 1987. *The Question of the Commons*. Tucson: University of Arizona Press.

McEvoy, Arthur. 1987. "Toward an Interactive Theory of Nature and Culture: Ecology, Production, and Cognition in the California Fishing Industry," *Environmental Review,* Vol. 11, No. 4, pp. 289–305.

McGilchrist, Iain. 1995. "It's not so much thinking out what to do, it's the doing of it that sticks me," *London Review of Books,* November 2, pp. 28–29.

McIlroy, Anne. 1996. "Environmentalists fear turf war over endangered wildlife," *Toronto Globe and Mail,* October 1, A8.

Meadows, Donella and Dennis Meadows. 1972. *Limits to Growth*. Washington: Potomac Associates.

Meiksins Wood, Ellen. 1995. *Democracy Against Capitalism: Renewing Historical Materialism*. New York: Cambridge University Press.

Melville, Elinor. 1994. "Underdevelopment and Unsustainability in Historical Perspective." In *Human Society and the Natural World*. David V.J. Bell, Roger Keil, and Gerda Wekerle [Eds.]. York University: Faculty of Environmental Studies, pp. 14–19.

Micale, Mark S. 1995. *Approaching Hysteria: Disease and Its Interpretations*. Princeton: Princeton University Press.

Mitchell, Bruce. 1989. *Geography and Resource Analysis*. New York: Longman and Wiley.

Morris, Jim. 1996. "B.C. fishermen get slap in face," *Winnipeg Free Press,* June 27, A2.

Mosquin, Theodore. 1977. "Foreword." In *Proceedings of the Symposium on Canada's Threatened Species and Habitats*. Theodore Mosquin and Cecile Suchal [Eds.]. Ottawa: Canadian Nature Federation, pp. v–ix.

Murkowski, Frank. 1985. *Pacific Salmon Treaty Hearing before the Committee on Foreign Relations, United States Senate*. February 22. Washington: U.S. Government Printing Office.

Nelson, Benjamin. 1969. *The Idea of Usury*. Chicago: University of Chicago Press.

Norman, Howard A.[collector and translator]. 1976. *The Wishing Bone Cycle: Narrative Poems from the Swampy Cree Indians*. New York: Stonehill, p. 100.

Ong, Aihwa. 1987. *Spirits of Resistance and Capitalist Discipline*. Albany: State University of New York Press.

Orr, David. 1994. *Earth in Mind: On Education, Environment, and the Human Prospect*. Washington: Island Press.

Orr, David. 1994. "Love It or Lose It: The Coming Biophilia Revolution," *Orion*, Winter. pp. 8–15.

Panayotou, Theodore. 1993. *Green Markets: The Economics of Sustainable Development*. San Francisco: Institute for Contemporary Studies Press.

Plumwood, Val. 1995. "Human Vulnerability and the Experience of Being Prey," *Quadrant*, pp. 29–34.

Plumwood, Val. 1993. *Feminism and the Mastery of Nature*. New York: Routledge.

Polanyi, Karl. 1957. *The Great Transformation: The Political and Economic Origins of Our Time*. Boston: Beacon Press.

Pynn, Larry. 1996. "Canadian jump-start only hope for fish pact, Alaska says," *Vancouver Sun*, April 17, B1.

Ramsey, John. M, Harold R. Hungerford, and Trudi Volk. 1991. "A Technique for Analyzing Environmental Issues," *Journal of Environmental Education*, Spring. pp. 41–45.

Redclift, Michael. 1994. "Environmental Managerialism." In *Capitalism and Development*. Leslie Sklair [Ed.]. New York: Routledge, pp. 123–39.

Rees, William E. 1994. "Pressing Global Limits: Trade as the Appropriation of Carrying Capacity." In *Growth, Trade and Environmental Values*. Ted Schrecker and Jean Dalgleish [Eds.]. London, Ontario: Westminster Institute, pp. 29–56.

Richards, Paul. 1996. *Fighting For The Rain Forest: War, Youth and Resources in Sierra Leone*. Portsmouth: James Curry and Heineman.

Richardson, Mary, Joan Sherman, and Michael Gismondi. 1993. *Winning Back the Words*. Vancouver: Garamond Press.

Rogers, Raymond A. 1995. *The Oceans Are Emptying: Fish Wars and Sustainability*. Montreal: Black Rose Books.

Rogers, Raymond A. 1994. *Nature and the Crisis of Modernity: A Critique of Contemporary Discourse on Managing the Earth*. Montreal: Black Rose Books.

Rotstein, Abraham. 1986. "Technology and Alienation," *Ultimate Reality and Meaning,* Vol. 9, No. 1, pp. 4–16.

Rowe, Stan. 1990. *Home Place: Essays on Ecology*. Edmonton: NeWest Publishers.

Sachs, Wolfgang. 1996. "Neo-Development: 'Global Ecological Management'." In *The Case Against the Global Economy* Jerry Mander and Edward Goldsmith [Eds.]. San Francisco: Sierra Club Books, pp. 239–52.

Sachs, Wolfgang [Ed.]. 1992. *The Development Dictionary*. London: Zed Books.

Sahlins, Marshall. 1985. *Islands of History*. Chicago: University of Chicago Press.

Sass, Louis. 1992. *Madness and Modernism: Insanity in the Light of Modern Art, Literature, and Thought*. New York: Basic Books.

Savage, Candace. 1989. "Foreword." In *On the Brink: Endangered Species in Canada*. A. Burnett, C.T. Dauphine, S.H. McCrindle, and T. Mosquin [Eds.]. Saskatoon: Western Producer Praire Books, p. vii.

Scott, James C. 1976. *The Moral Economy of the Peasant: Rebellion, and Subsistence in Southeast Asia*. New Haven: Yale University Press.

Shakespeare, William. 1931. *King Lear*. Hardin Craig [Ed.]. New York: Scott, Foresman & Co.

Shiva, Vandana. 1993. *Monocultures of the Mind: Perspectives on Biodiversity and Biotechnology*. London: Zed Books.

Showalter, Elaine. 1997. *Hystories: Hysterical Epidemics and Modern Media*. New York: Colombia University Press.

Simmel, Georg. *The Philosophy of Money*. David Frisby [Ed.]. New York: Routledge.

Simpson, Jeffrey. 1997. "It's time Newfoundland took a brave stand on its fish industry," *Toronto Globe and Mail,* September 18, A18.

Skogstad, Grace; Kopas, Paul. 1992. "Environmental Policy in a Federal System: Ottawa and the Provinces." In *Canadian Environmental Policy: Ecosystems, Politics, and Process* Robert Boardman [Ed.]. Toronto: Oxford University Press, pp. 43–59.

Soulé, Michael. 1986. "Conservation Biology and the Real World." In *Conservation Biology: The Science of Scarcity and Diversity*. Michael Soulé [Ed.]. Sunderland: Sinauer Associates.

Tawny, R.H. 1980. *Religion and the Rise of Capitalism*. Harmondsworth: Penguin.

Tawny, R.H. 1925. "Introduction" to *A Discourse Upon Usury*, by Thomas Wilson. New York: Harcourt Brace, pp. 1–172.

Taussig, Michael. 1992. *The Nervous System*. New York: Routledge.

Temple, Dominique. 1988. "The Policy of the Severed Flower," *INTERculture*, Vol. 98. Winter, pp. 10–35.

Thompson, E.P. 1978. "Folklore, Anthropology, and Social History," *Indian Historical Review*, Vol. 3, No. 2, pp. 247–66.

Thompson, E.P. 1971. "The Moral Economy of the English Crowd in the Eighteenth Century." *Past and Present*, No. 50, pp. 76–136.

Thompson, E.P. 1967. "Time, Work-Discipline, and Industrial Capitalism," *Past and Present*, No. 38, pp. 56–97.

Toronto Globe and Mail [Editor]. 1997. "What farmers could teach the fishery," *The Toronto Globe and Mail*, October 9, A18.

Walters, Carl. 1995. *Fish on the Line: The Future of Pacific Fisheries*. Vancouver: The David Suzuki Foundation.

Wellington, Alex. 1997. "Endangered Species Policy: Ethics, Politics, Science and Law." In *Canadian Issues in Environmental Ethics*. Alex Wellington, Allan Greenbaum and Wesley Cragg [Eds.]. Toronto: Broadview Press, pp. 189–218.

Williams, Raymond. 1980. "Ideas of Nature." In *Problems in Materialism and Culture*. New York: Verso, pp. 67–85.

World Conservation Strategy. 1980. Gland: IUCN, UNEP, WWF.

Worster, Donald. 1993. "The Shakey Ground of Sustainability." In *Global Ecology: A New Arena of Political Conflict*. Wolfgang Sachs [Ed.]. London: Zed Books.

Index